WHO'S ON TOP, WHO'S ON BOTTOM

ALSO BY THE AUTHOR

*Saying No Is Not Enough: Raising Children
Who Make Wise Decisions About Drugs and Alcohol*

A Guide to a Happier Family (coauthor)

WHO'S ON TOP, WHO'S ON BOTTOM

How Couples Can Learn to Share Power

Robert Schwebel, Ph.D.

Newmarket Press
New York

*To my parents, Milton and Bernice, who taught me about love
and inspired me with their loving relationship,
and to Claudia, my wife and partner in love,
with whom I hope to inspire our children, Frank and Henry.*

Copyright © 1994 by Robert Schwebel, Ph.D.

This book published simultaneously in the United States of America and in Canada.
All rights reserved. This book may not be reproduced, in whole or in part, in any form,
without written permission. Inquiries should be addressed to
Permissions Department, Newmarket Press,
18 East 48th Street, New York, NY 10017.

94 95 96 97   10 9 8 7 6 5 4 3 2 1

Library of Congress Cataloging-in-Publication Data
Schwebel, Robert.
Who's on top, who's on bottom: how couples can learn
to share power/ Robert Schwebel.—1st ed.
p.   cm.
ISBN 1-55704-197-0
1. Marriage.   2. Cooperation.   3. Communication in marriage.
I.   Title.
HQ734.S418   1994
646.7'8—dc20   93-46313
                                           CIP

QUANTITY PURCHASES
Companies, professional groups, clubs, and other organizations may qualify for special
terms when ordering quantities of this title. For information, write
Special Sales Department, Newmarket Press, 18 East 48th Street,
New York, NY 10017, or call (212) 832-3575.

Manufactured in the United States of America
FIRST EDITION

Newmarket Press books by Robert Schwebel, Ph.D.:

*Saying No Is Not Enough: Raising Children
Who Make Wise Decisions About Drugs and Alcohol*

Who's on Top, Who's on Bottom: How Couples Can Learn to Share Power

INTRODUCTION

I am pleased to have the opportunity to welcome the reader to this helpful and incisive book.

In *Who's on Top, Who's on Bottom*, Dr. Schwebel steers clear of the dogmas that have grown up in the field of family and couples therapy. Instead, he maintains that competition, and the need for one member of a couple to exercise power over the other, is the principal source of couples' dysfunction. Emphasizing that we grow up in a competitive society that values winning, he argues that many of the difficulties that bring couples to therapy can be traced to this underlying struggle. But Dr. Schwebel does not remain on this abstract level. Instead, he effectively uses concrete examples from his practice and from his own life to illustrate the principles he has derived for understanding a couple's conflict and assisting them in maintaining and improving their relationship.

Without indulging in jargon, Dr. Schwebel has used real-life examples to illustrate the behaviors he has identified as the major reasons for tension in couples. He has also labeled the attitudes and actions that can lead to solving continuing conflicts. Thus, he refers to a "BCA"—a Basic Cooperative Agreement—as a useful starting point in helping couples resolve differences and foster a relationship not based on power plays. He has terms to describe both the impasses that couples experience ("locking horns," "stuck points," for example) and the positive behaviors that overcome these impasses ("super decisions," "huddling up," to name two). The reader is introduced to these terms in the context of case discussions and can refer to them again in the explanatory glossary that constitutes the last chapter of the book. Further, the author offers no Pollyanna conclusion that all conflicts are resolvable by all couples; some of the examples are of couples who ultimately divorced.

Dr. Schwebel has succeeded in making theory practical, and in illustrating therapeutic approaches in ways that appeal to both a lay and a professional audience. *Who's on Top, Who's on Bottom* is accessible to the individual seeking greater understanding of conflicts and their resolution and illuminating for the professional, providing new insights and food for thought.

This is an interesting and provocative book that deserves a wide and enthusiastic readership.

Cynthia P. Deutsch, Ph.D.
Professor and Chair
Department of Applied Psychology
New York University

CONTENTS

Chapter 1	Who's on Top, Who's on Bottom	11
Chapter 2	Love Story	33
Chapter 3	The Cooperative Vision	53
Chapter 4	Dominance and Submission	68
Chapter 5	Super Skills	85
Chapter 6	Stuck Point	100
Chapter 7	Locked Horns	116
Chapter 8	Loving Communication	131
Chapter 9	On-Track and Off-Track Communication	161
Chapter 10	Cooperative Negotiation	182
Chapter 11	Unconscious Barriers to Intimacy and Cooperation	214
Chapter 12	Glossary/Summary of Ideas	236

PREFACE

Many of the ideas in this book came from experience rather than research. I was fortunate to have grown up with excellent role models. My parents, Milton and Bernice—happily married for fifty-four years now—showed me how a couple can lovingly take care of each other. My mother always told me, "What's good for the goose is good for the gander." My father showed me how real men—loving men—behave.

It's important to put ideas into practice. I've been joyfully doing this with my wife Claudia. We've learned much from each other. I hope our happy marriage will inspire our children to also have loving, wonderful marriages when their time comes.

I am able to write about people learning to love because in the last twenty-five years I have counseled so many individuals and couples who have worked to create good relationships. I owe a debt of gratitude to the people who have trusted me as their psychologist, opened up, and improved their own lives. I have learned a great deal from them.

Psychological research on the topic of cooperation has influenced the development of my thinking. My colleagues in the San Francisco Bay Area helped inspire many of the ideas on sharing power as equals. I owe a special thanks to Claude Steiner who was my mentor in the art of therapy. I also want to thank Becky Jenkins, Beth Roy, and Michael Singer.

I am grateful to Samuel Baskin who gave me my first opportunity to write professionally. Back in graduate school days, Philip Cowan was an important source of support. I owe a great deal to my good friend Leo Banks who helped start me as a journalist and showed me the ropes. Nadine Epstein helped me develop my writing style, in particular, helping me discover my preference for a story-telling approach. Another good friend, Mark Turner, also helped me as a writer.

My dear friends Brian McCaffrey and Sylvia Yee read two of the early chapters of this book and made helpful suggestions. I want to thank other friends: Craig Wunderlich, Alex Zautra, Marilyn Civer, Martha McEwen and Don Oberthur, Barbara Brown and David Boomhower, Benjamin Spock and Mary Morgan, Mike and Susie Cohen, Bob Calhoun, Teresa Banks, and Jeri and Richard Briskin. Also I thank my in-laws, the Genda family, for their support.

Thanks to Andrew Schwebel for a lifetime of older brother support for my work, and special mention to his family: Carol, Davy, and Sara. Also due credit are other inspirational forces, namely my grandparents: Joseph and Sara Davison, and Frank and Sarah Schwebel.

Behind the scenes all through the writing of this book was a sensitive, intelligent, and supportive editor: Keith Hollaman. He made several suggestions that substantially improved this work. He has also been an advocate for this book from start to finish. I am very thankful for his extraordinary help.

I also thank Al Zuckerman of Writer's House and Esther Margolis of Newmarket Press for their continued support and confidence.

* * *

All of the characters and incidents in this book are fictional, although they are based on the author's experience as a psychologist. They realistically depict the type of problems that couples in therapy face.

CHAPTER

1

Who's on Top, Who's on Bottom

For years Ken had pooh-poohed marriage therapy. "People need to work out their own problems," he said to his wife, Helen, "without paying someone to tell them what to do."

"And if *you're* so unhappy," he continued, "*you* should go get help for yourself. But don't drag me along. I'm not gonna see a shrink."

Ken wouldn't budge. This was nonnegotiable. So Helen continued to complain about their relationship . . . without the benefit of professional help.

"You promise to do something," Helen would say, "and then never follow through. I can't depend on you. I have to do things myself to make sure that they get done right.

"And you don't seem to want to be close. You won't talk with me. I never know what you feel. I'm sick of it."

To bolster her efforts at improving their marriage, Helen devoured one self-help book after another. She followed the prescribed advice and sometimes managed to get Ken to read a few pages and try some of the techniques. They learned a variety of communication, negotiation, and relationship skills. But they did not get the quick fix of marital happiness that these books so often promised.

Despite all her own hard work and Ken's generally reluctant efforts, Helen still felt dissatisfied. She still felt that something was missing. The problem was deeper.

Finally, after years of contemplating divorce, Helen made the leap. She threatened to leave . . . and meant it. It was not easy to take this step. They had started with great love for each other. They still shared many similar interests and could have fun together when they were not arguing. Most of all, they had produced two wonderful children. Helen worried about the impact of a divorce on their kids.

But husband and wife had been drifting apart, spending less and less time together. Over the years, Ken had become increasingly silent and withdrawn. The last straw occurred when Helen realized that they had not made love in almost three months, including a week-long vacation in the Caribbean without their children. She wanted more in a marriage and seemed to be getting less.

When Ken realized that Helen meant business about divorce, they eventually ended up in my office, seeking help. Suddenly marriage counseling was negotiable.

In most ways this couple resembles many of the couples with whom I have worked in the past twenty-five years. They wanted love. They wanted closeness. They were good people. They started with good feelings and excitement about each other but could not successfully maintain their positive feelings. Each person became dissatisfied with the other and with the relationship. Their affection diminished.

Helen initially had been attracted to Ken because he was so nice. She had grown up with an angry, aggressive father, and liked that Ken was gentle, "laid back," and inoffensive. He basically avoided conflict. In fact, he was quite passive and tended to let external circumstances dictate his life.

Ken's passivity extended to his view of relationships. He believed that relationships either succeeded or didn't, depending on whether you had chosen the right partner. He thought that good relationships "just happened" without effort, and that they would be free of conflict. In his mind, strife of any sort meant that something was basically wrong. So when Helen and he argued, Ken thought he had made a mistake in choosing his partner. He resented Helen. But he was too passive to try to fix things, and also too passive to think about breaking up and starting again with someone else. Ken maintained the relationship by increasing his distance. He kept busy with friends, and with various hobbies and recreational activities.

Helen, on the other hand, knew that relationships require effort. She was willing to work hard—so much so that she pushed her resistant husband into reading parts of self-help books. But what she didn't realize was that all of her pushing was just breeding resentment.

Although neither would describe it this way, the two of them were locked in a power struggle. Helen felt that she was trying to get Ken to grow up, be responsible, and learn what constitutes a good relationship. Ken didn't readily admit to his complaints, but he basically felt that Helen was a bossy woman who wanted to tell him how to lead his life. When he was really angry, he sarcastically called her "the colonel."

The love stories in this book, including this particular one, have unfolded in my clinical practice of psychology as women and men reveal their struggles with one another. The core of each story is about people in relationships who love each other but are engaged in power struggles and *unable to share power as equals*. In our culture, people learn to feel comfortable on top, or on bottom, or in a power struggle for the top position. They either abuse power or give it away. Some couples *appear* to avoid power struggles, comfortably fitting together with one person dominating and the other submitting. In the long run, however, this pattern is unstable. Eventually submissive people resent that their love and kindness are not reciprocated. They say, "I've done so much for you, why don't you do more for me?" And then the power struggle commences.

Most people do not realize the extent of the power struggle in their relationship, unless perhaps it has escalated to the point where they are practically throwing kitchen chairs at each other. Many individuals see themselves as fair, cooperative people trying to deal with unreasonable or mistaken partners. They think of their own complaints as an effort to "right a wrong."

"If only my partner would (fill in the blank), then our relationship would be better."

They try to "fix" their partners to save the marriage. Helen was doing this with Ken.

Other people in power struggles think that they are merely defending themselves or trying to hold their ground against an aggressive or overbearing partner whom they believe is harming them in some way. They don't want to be cheated or mistreated. Ken thought of himself in this way—simply fighting against Helen in self-defense.

WHERE DID IT BEGIN?

Ken and Helen had started with love and excitement. Having much in common was a head start. It meant fewer disagreements. But no two people—even the most compatible— want the same things all the time. Conflict is part of life and part of every relationship.

In their early days together, Ken and Helen barely noticed differences. Each was on best behavior. Both were so excited about being a couple that they tended to overlook problems. Of course, they had occasional disagreements; some they could resolve, and others were brushed aside.

Yet over time, Helen and Ken had slipped into a competitive mode, arguing about who was right and who was wrong, and struggling to see which of them would prevail. Both were convinced that their viewpoints were right and the other's were wrong. Each communicated to win. Each negotiated to win. They sometimes said things or did things in anger that did not reflect the caring feelings they felt for each other. They lost sight of the loving spirit of a relationship.

Ken and Helen lacked what most people I see in therapy lack, namely, a vision of cooperatively sharing power. Ken and Helen had no idea how a couple could stay close when the going gets rough, and no awareness that it is possible to remain a team and to solve problems together.

First and foremost, this book is about that *vision of cooperatively sharing power.*

Grasping and embracing this vision is a huge challenge. The vision runs totally counter to the enormous emphasis and tremendous value put on competitiveness in our society. We are thoroughly programmed to compete and to feel comfortable in power-based relationships—one person on top and the other on bottom. We tend to approach conflict as adversaries pitted against one another. We see the world as either I win and you lose, or you win and I lose. Or we hope to sidestep a power struggle by trying to avoid all conflict. In the long run, this eventually leads to even more trouble.

Most couples start well. In the name of love, people can suspend at least some selfishness and competitiveness as they form relationships. But when problems arise, couples lack a vision of how to stick together. Competitive tendencies surface, just as they did in Helen and Ken's relationship. Fear and insecurity take over as people revert to what they have learned so well: how to compete.

It is clear that relationship problems are much more than deficiencies in skills and techniques. Skills and techniques are necessary, but not sufficient for creating fully satisfying relationships. No simple recipes and quick fixes will solve basic problems. The core issue is deeper: the very vision of what it means to be a couple.

Who's on Top, Who's on Bottom is not a relationship manual of "ten easy steps" to instant happiness. What you will find instead is a vision and an attitude to guide action, and within this context, some methods and skills for sharing power cooperatively. You will see that learning to share power as equals is an exercise in self-discipline, trust, patience, and skill-building.

Instead of giving advice, the following chapters will paint pictures to portray a vision of couples learning to share power as equals. You will read about couples such as Helen and Ken, some of whom succeed in their endeavor, and some who do not. These love stories depict the real struggles that couples face, conveying the scope and depth of problems that they confront, and the vision, attitudes, and skills that are needed to build and maintain satisfying love relationships.

In the context of these love stories, I present certain concepts to think about if you want to establish and stay on track with a cooperative attitude. I also suggest some techniques that can help you develop the skills needed to back up this vision of sharing power as equals.

SUCCESSFUL COUPLES

In the love stories, some of the individuals are more attuned to their partner's needs than others, and better able to express their love. Some of them, compared to others, are better able to handle conflict. Regardless, all the couples start with a positive exchange. They want to be together. They want to make each other happy. Most couples are able to resolve at least some of their conflict. Some are able to resolve most of their conflict.

Sooner or later, however, each couple is tested. They discover substantial differences that don't lend themselves to easy solutions. These differences can develop into a crisis.

The couples may have serious misunderstandings and substantial conflict. They might stop talking or get caught in repetitive fights with the same stuck point. They get suspicious and become mistrustful. They lock horns. They compete for power or settle into a dominant/submissive pattern that creates serious problems. They cannot share power as equals and are unable to work as a team to find solutions to problems that satisfy both partners. More and more they start to see their own needs in conflict with their partner's. The good feelings and goodwill diminish. They lose sight of their love and become increasingly bitter and angry.

To put these relationship crises in context, I like to talk about successful "sunset couples." These are couples who have been together happily for many years, and are walking arm in arm toward the sunset of life. I have interviewed many of these couples. Almost without exception they talk about having had tough times at some point in their relationship. But somehow they navigated the troubled waters and found happiness together. It is noteworthy that most of them point to the same lessons.

The sunset couples discuss the great importance they placed on talking through their differences, no matter how late they stayed up at night or how long the dialogue lasted. Sometimes discussions continued for weeks and even months. Ultimately they were *able to find solutions to conflict that satisfied both partners*.

The sunset couples also spoke about the importance of *tolerance* at times when they inadvertently hurt each other, and of the necessity of *calmly communicating*, even when hurt or angry about something. It's not that these couples were perfect. But when they made mistakes, they made amends and tried to learn from their experiences. In other words, the sunset couples discovered how to take care of each other and how to share power as equals.

Even these highly successful couples admit that it is a struggle to create a satisfying relationship. It is an uphill battle. In a sense, we are all headed for trouble with our relationships because our culture does not provide a realistic model for success. To succeed in sharing power, we have to transcend the dominant model for relationships in our culture: competition.

In each case in this book, you will read about couples who need to develop a solid, cooperative spirit that will hold up when they are tense, upset, confused, or in conflict. They need to learn to share power as equals. Ultimately they need to see clearly that they are in a relationship to take care of each other and hold steadfast to this goal.

THE FIRST SESSION

Helen had been waiting a long time to get to a counseling session, so she had plenty to say. She presented a strong case about Ken's shortcomings, starting with a substantial list of complaints about times he said he would do something and then failed to follow through, including speaking to his boss about promotions, doing household repairs, caring for their children, and paying bills. Helen was fed up with Ken's broken promises and had concluded he simply was undependable.

Even Ken did not protest against these complaints.

At one point he did get a little defensive and pointed out that he had painted the garage just a few weeks ago, as he had promised. He said he was getting better and more reliable.

"But even that," Helen said, "is an example of what I'm talking about. You told me you would paint the garage eight months ago. I had to remind you countless times."

Next Helen started talking about "not having a relationship." She gave a long list of examples of Ken's inadequacies in intimacy: He didn't want to spend time with her, rarely initiated making love, didn't talk much about his daily life, and gave very few compliments. He only infrequently asked her about *her* preferences when they made plans.

Ken again did not try to counter her examples, but attempted to defend himself by mentioning the week they had just spent in the Caribbean: "You were the one who wanted to do that. You were always saying I never spend special time with you. But if you think about it I do almost everything you want. You get your way most of the time in this marriage. You always have.

"I don't fight you anymore," he continued. "I've given up. These days I do the things you want more than ever. The trip to the Caribbean was entirely your idea, and I went along. But you still aren't happy. I can't ever do enough."

"Well," Helen answered, "it was during this last trip that I realized how bad things are between us. We had baby-sitting for the kids. We had time alone, which, you are right, I had been wanting for ages. And look what happened: You barely spoke to me. You seemed grumpy the whole time. We didn't even make love once."

"Maybe," Ken answered, "it's because you always want to be on top."

I intervened at this point because it was clear that they were about to lose control, and a discussion about sexual intimacy would not be productive.

Tensions gradually cooled in the next few minutes. All in all, Ken agreed with many of Helen's complaints. He said he realized that she was serious about divorce and that he would start delivering the changes he had been promising for so long.

But something was wrong. It was too simple. Ken was too agreeable. His comment about not fighting Helen anymore subtly undermined his apparent surrender. And you could hear his resentment just below the surface.

"There's no change here," Helen said. "Ken will agree to everything I want. But he won't follow through. You watch. He doesn't know what it means to make a commitment."

"I went to the Caribbean, didn't I?"

In this exchange, Helen's critical comment about Ken's inability to make a commitment had prompted a defensive response about their trip and started another round of argument. In the end it was clear to me. Helen wanted the Caribbean trip. Ken didn't. He went along, resented it, and didn't give her what she wanted, which was closeness. Helen was hurt, and resented Ken. Neither of them really got what they wanted. It was a lose-lose situation.

GIVING IN/TAKING OVER

At one point in the session Ken had said that he would talk with Helen every day, right after work, just as she had requested. She wanted "personal talks," and he agreed.

"Are you going to do that?" I asked.

"Yes," he said, "I know it's important."

"Do you really want to do that?" I asked.

"I guess so," he said unenthusiastically. "It's okay."

"Please," I said, "think about whether you *want* to do it. Do you feel like it?"

"Not really. But she wants it. I *have to* give her what I say I'm going to do. I need to do it. She's right. We need more intimacy, and I've promised to deliver, and haven't."

"And if you don't do it?"

"She'll bitch and complain at me." He paused. "I'd better do things her way or I'm in trouble. It's been the story of our relationship. Now I think she'll leave me if I don't follow through."

You didn't have to dig deep to find his resentment. Ken felt bullied. At the same time, he conceded that most of Helen's complaints had merit. He agreed that he had been derelict at following through. He also admitted that Helen and he were lacking in intimacy.

As we continued, I discovered that "personal talks" after work had been a long-standing source of conflict between them. Ken had agreed to these talks previously, but never kept his promise. With much prodding in our session, Ken revealed his own thoughts and feelings on the matter. He said he was less inclined toward personal openness than Helen. He also usually liked to relax alone at home first, before getting together with his family.

"You never told me that," Helen commented.

Ken said he never spelled it out in "black and white" before but that he had alluded to it. When he once mentioned spending a little time alone after work, Helen told him he had "no idea how a good family works." So nowadays he said, "I've learned to keep my mouth shut."

By this time, the rough contour of the conflict of their personalities was beginning to unfold.

Helen was an outspoken, takeover person. She had clear ideas about how things should be done. She knew what she wanted and would say so. She was strong, sometimes assertive, and sometimes pushy and dogmatic.

Ken was more relaxed about things, sometimes lax. Although he had thoughts and opinions, he was passive and did not feel free to express them. When it was time to make a decision, he would respond to Helen's initiative rather than taking an initiative of his own.

They both were angry at each other. They had learned communication techniques, but whenever they talked it was always with a tone of anger and bitterness.

THE POWER STRUGGLE

The seesaw power dynamic in their relationship was beginning to show.

When they disagreed, Helen started on top because Ken deferred to her wishes. He felt that she was in charge and that he had to do things her way. Although he willingly gave away his power, his resentment about her dominance was evident. Also, he was not fully committed to "her" plans and often failed to follow through. Or he did what he promised, but with bitterness. By not doing what he said he would do, or doing it resentfully, Ken found a passive way to fight back. He was briefly on top. But not for long.

Helen countered by calling him "irresponsible." She also doubted his love: "If he really loved me," she said, "he would show it by doing what he said he was going to do." She was angry and critical. She said Ken didn't know how to love anyone. She also took matters into her own hands by doing whatever Ken had said he was going to do, and doing it right. In the end, she got the job done.

Ken kind of accepted Helen's characterization of him as irresponsible (because he did not do what he promised), but also resented her criticism of him. He saw Helen as an angry, controlling person. He thought, "If she loved me, she wouldn't criticize me all the time." He also hated it when she "took over" and did things her own way. Sometimes he would sabotage her plans. When one of her initiatives failed—as in a bad investment—he would be quick to point it out. Also, in anger, Ken sometimes hurt Helen by withdrawing his affection.

This couple had give-and-take. The power was fairly equal, but they were not sharing it. There was no cooperation. They were adversaries. She was on top for a while, then he, then she. It always felt bad. Each was wrestling power away from the other one. They could not enjoy their time together. Both lost in this arrangement. Neither person got what was really wanted. Each felt angry and distant from the other. Both complained that the other did not make them feel special.

He said, "Helen is always critical and angry. She takes over."

She said, "Ken is always distant and angry. I can't count on him."

I talked with them about the ways they had locked horns, each person doing something that made matters worse.

His power was passive: withdrawing from Helen, withholding affection, and not doing what he said he would do.

Her power was overt: taking control and criticizing Ken in a variety of ways.

The more he was passive, the more she criticized him ("not capable of intimacy" and "not doing what he said he would do"), and the more she took over (getting him to read self-help books; getting him to travel to the Caribbean; and nagging him to finish tasks he had said he would do, or finishing the tasks herself). However, the more she criticized and controlled, the more he rebelled by not doing what he said, or by doing it with hostility and bitterness, and by withdrawing his affection (as on the Caribbean trip, and by spending most of his time with hobbies and friends). It was a vicious circle.

This was their pattern with many issues. Ken was passive. Helen took control. During various sessions I found that Ken felt he had to handle financial matters the way Helen wanted, do household repairs on her schedule, fight for promotions at work the way she would like it done, and plan parties the way she wanted them. Helen complained that Ken didn't do what he said, or did it resentfully, and that he was always pushing her away.

Sometimes Ken appreciated Helen's initiative. But in general, he resented her dominance. Often he agreed with her point of view. But when he occasionally objected, she would outtalk him, and he would accede to her wishes.

CONCESSIONS

In the heat of battle, both Ken and Helen thought they were being cooperative and trying to make the relationship work. At the moment when Ken would agree to do something, he thought he was being a good husband—a peacemaker—by giving his wife what she wanted. At the time he made commitments, he intended to follow through.

When Ken *didn't*, Helen would think she was fixing the marriage by teaching him about responsibility and commitment. She also felt that she was saving the day by taking matters into her own hands.

These are common misconceptions about cooperation in relationships. People think they are being cooperative when they make concessions, such as "I'll give in (and let her boss me around)" or "I'll take over (and do all the work)." But it is not really cooperative to give in begrudgingly to a partner, nor is it cooperative to resentfully carry more than a fair share of responsibilities. When Helen and Ken interacted in this way, each felt unloved. Each felt angry.

Through our sessions they began to realize that making concessions is not the same as cooperative compromise, which is based on good discussion (including input from both individuals) and mutual respect. With cooperative compromise, people meet each other halfway, or make trade-offs in the spirit of "my way this time and your way next time." Cooperative compromise is done with grace and good feelings toward a partner. Helen and Ken had nothing but resentment.

TWO ANGRY PEOPLE

"Look," I told Ken and Helen at one of our early sessions, "you two are like every other couple. You have disagreements and conflict. You have different ideas about the priority that should be given to household repairs, the way your money is invested, what you do at the end of the workday, how you throw parties, how you will be close with one another, and lots of other issues. The problem isn't the disagreements. We all have them. The problem is how you handle them.

"You don't have good discussions and negotiations. You don't know how to share power. Ken, you give away your power. You're not good at putting forward your point of view. And you back down too quickly. Helen, you push ahead with your own ideas without finding out where Ken stands. You take power without Ken's participation. Ken doesn't *really* buy into your ideas, and then you're angry at him when he doesn't follow through."

Passive as he tended to be, Ken liked that I was pointing out Helen's participation in their problems. He took advantage of this and chimed in about how hard it is to live with a partner who is always angry and critical.

He was surprised when I said I thought he was equally angry and critical. "You're no pushover," I said. "You show your anger by not doing what you say you will do, or by doing it late or resentfully. You know how to make Helen angry. And you also show your anger by withdrawing your affection from her. Don't you?"

"And," I added, "listen to yourself: Given an opportunity, you are very critical of Helen."

Ken admitted it was true, and as we talked even added that sometimes he spent time with friends just to make her angry. He also admitted that sometimes he withheld sex to make her feel bad.

As our sessions continued, they began to see that the agreements they made were not a team effort with input by both individuals. Rather they were the result of Helen's pushiness and Ken's passivity. Both were angry.

A COOPERATIVE VISION

I pointed out to Helen and Ken that they had been competing and wasting their energy in bitter adversarial confrontations. Both felt hurt and unloved. I said the tension would persist until they broke this pattern of a seesaw power struggle.

During the first couple of sessions, we talked about a cooperative vision of couples sharing power as equals. Instead of struggling against one another, couples can define their problems as mutual. Cooperative couples approach conflict by saying, "How are we going to settle this particular difference—whatever it might be—so that we both are satisfied with the outcome?" This means that they would be a team looking for mutually satisfying solutions. Solutions would not be "my way" or "your way"; rather, they would be "our way."

In the sessions, we talked at length about win-win negotiations, in which everyone feels good. You either get exactly what you wanted, or a fair compromise, or you make a trade-off. Couples can tell when they have a cooperative solution: Each person can smile at the other and say, "This may not be exactly what I wanted, but we talked it out fully and fairly, and it feels right."

RECOMMENDATION FOR MAKING PEACE

Both Helen and Ken had focused on the wrongdoing of the other person. As you will see in the love stories in this book, most people see their relationship problems as being caused by their partners. They have a clear idea about their partners' flaws but do not see their own contribution to problems. I explained to Helen and Ken that they could not change each other, but could make changes together that would increase the harmony of their relationship. I urged them to think about their own responsibility—what they were doing as individuals that prevented them from cooperatively sharing power.

Over the next several sessions I stated, clarified, and restated a set of recommendations for each of them:

For Ken:
- Always express your point of view.
- Say what you want.
- Don't back down so quickly.
- Catch yourself when you make excuses to give in, such as, "She won't listen to my opinions; she'll do things her way anyway."
- Stick up for yourself if you feel your feelings and thoughts are not respected.
- When something bothers you, say so. Don't withdraw.
- Don't agree to do something unless it feels right.
- Do what you say you are going to do, and do it without resentment.

- If Helen starts to "take over," respectfully start a dialogue about what you think is happening.

For Helen:
- Ask Ken to say what he thinks and feels.
- Let Ken give his opinions first, at least half the time.
- Listen respectfully to Ken's point of view.
- Do not make an agreement unless Ken has clearly stated where he stands.
- If you disagree with Ken, engage in a dialogue. State your thoughts and feelings, and ask him to clarify his.
- If Ken does not do what he said he would do, respectfully start a dialogue to ascertain and correct the cause of the problem.
- Don't make excuses for taking over, such as, "Ken won't do what he said. It won't get done right unless I do it."
- Don't take over.

I put all these recommendations in context by introducing Helen and Ken to cooperative negotiation. I told them that everything has to be on the table for couples to settle conflict. People have to know the starting points—what each other thinks—to find common ground, and also to find the middle point for compromise: "Once you know what each other thinks and feels, you can begin looking for solutions that will feel okay to both of you."

I said, especially to Ken, that it is important to accept that conflict is a normal part of relationships. It is not always easy to find solutions, but the only possible way to succeed is by bringing differences into the open and talking respectfully. If there is no discussion, there will be no solutions.

I also told Ken and Helen that they had to *trust the process*—that is, believe that people can lovingly look at their differences and together find solutions that will satisfy both people. At this point I said, "Take my word." I was aware that they had never had cooperative role models, but told them that, without question, people can share power as equals. It requires effort, trust, self-discipline, and also a leap of faith that a better way exists.

Part of trusting the process is believing in your partner. We all have flaws. In particular, none of us is great at sharing power. Ultimately we have to believe that we and our partners will do our best to correct our own errors. In their case, it meant that Helen would be more interested in Ken's point of view and would not "take over." Ken would more assertively bring his thoughts and feelings into discussions. He would do what he said he was going to do, and not withdraw when he was angry. Helen had to believe that Ken could be "responsible." Ken had to believe that Helen did not want to control him. It was a tall order.

RELATIONSHIP LEADER

When I first proposed this new way to think about sharing power, both Helen and Ken pessimistically focused on the other person. Ken said, "She'll never back off. She just wants to control me."

Helen said, "I've proposed this before. He won't say what he thinks, and he won't do what he says. He doesn't understand commitment. He doesn't know how to have a relationship."

"Listen to her," Ken said. "No wonder I don't do things for her. She's always angry. She always has to have the final word."

"See?" she replied. "I can't count on him."

I couldn't have scripted it better. I told them that they were doing right then and there what I had been talking about. Each was doubting the other. Neither person was willing to go first.

I said, "Someone has to be a *relationship leader*. Instead of waiting for the other person to change, why don't you do what you actually have the power to do: deal with your part of the problem?"

I said it is like jumping into a cold swimming pool with a friend. Both people have to go. It works best when both jump together, especially if they hold hands as they jump. But someone has to start by saying "Let's count to three." Or someone has to jump in and believe that the other will follow. If the other doesn't follow, at least the first one gets a good swim.

"The only way I can see that you will improve your relationship is if you both change your roles. One of you can be the leader to inspire the other. But if you wait around and doubt your partner, nothing will ever change."

Certainly they had established a pattern that led them to doubt each other. But, I argued, that pattern could be corrected.

LEAPING TOGETHER

Helen and Ken started by putting their toes in the water, and then made the leap. They began to see their own part in the relationship problems, and were willing to change. I think they realized they were on the verge of losing the relationship if they didn't do something drastic.

Unfortunately, it is often easier to see what needs to be done than to do it. Old habits are hard to shake. Time and again Helen and Ken repeated the familiar pattern in one situation after another. Typically Helen would take over or Ken would not do what he promised. The other person would then revert to the old practices. When Ken didn't do what he said he would do, Helen would take over and criticize him as if he were a child. When Helen criticized and took over, Ken would angrily withdraw.

Change is slow. Couples have to repeat their errors over and over again until the pattern becomes clear: Oops, we did it there. Oops, we did it again. Eventually there is a significant shift. Each person gets better at not falling into the old roles. When one person does fall, the other gets better at not making a complementary mistake that would compound the problem.

The rule of thumb is simple: If one person blows it (we are all imperfect), it is important that the other one doesn't blow it, too. Why? Because then it would become a major fight.

Helen and Ken worked at "cuing" each other back on course when one person would revert to the old roles. When Ken thought Helen was taking over, he would *not* withdraw. Instead he would tell her what he observed, and they would have a discussion. When Ken didn't do what he said he would, Helen would *not* take over. Instead she would point it out respectfully, and ask what was happening.

Always they aimed for the same bottom line: to get calm so they could have reasoned discussions with a cooperative spirit. They faced a big challenge. They needed to settle so many issues that had remained unsettled because of their competitive styles. Slowly they worked through the many issues that had troubled them.

AUTOMATIC PROCESSING

I warned Helen and Ken to be alert for what is known as *automatic processing*. This is part of spiraling negativity in relationships. What happens is, people in relationships see their partners in certain ways. They expect and look for certain behavior and do not see behavior that differs from what they expect. They process information automatically, without much conscious control. Helen expected Ken would not do what he said. Ken expected Helen would take over. They had lots of assumptions about each other.

Even as they talked through many differences and slowly made progress in their relationship, they kept coming face to face with automatic thinking.

At one session, we were discussing emotional intimacy. They realized they needed to agree on how to be close.

Ken had admitted that he sometimes withdrew from Helen as a way to show his anger. He had been doing less of that. In the past, Helen had repeatedly pressured Ken to show closeness the way she liked it shown. In particular, this meant frequent sharing of emotions. The more she criticized him for his inability to be loving, the more he had withdrawn from her. In our sessions, they were working toward a definition of how they would show their closeness to one another. Ken said he showed closeness just by being with her, and felt close even if they were simply watching television or doing activities.

Inevitably the discussion shifted to sex. Helen complained that Ken was withholding sex as a way of acting out his anger. Ken admitted that he had sometimes done this in the past, but said that it was not the case now.

"Well, why don't you want to make love now?" she asked. "It must be you don't know how to be loving," she continued, with her automatic thinking.

"No, I disagree," Ken said. "I know how to be loving. I'm not exactly sure what's actually going on, but part of the problem is that you always want to be on top. I guess that now that we're finally learning to share power, I'll tell you the truth: I don't like it that you always insist on being on top."

"That's not even so," Helen answered. "When I just tell you what I like—for example, that I like being on top *sometimes*—you think I'm telling you how things have to be done all the time. That's not fair at all."

It turned out that this was Ken's automatic thinking. He was assuming that Helen's preference was a demand. He would comply, and then resent it.

As the discussion unfolded, Ken learned that Helen liked being on the top far less often than he had imagined. It turned out Ken had been doing what he *thought* Helen demanded, much more than he liked it, and in fact much more than even she liked it.

Maybe it was the symbolism of the top/bottom issue. I'm not sure. But somehow clearing up this misunderstanding led to a blossoming of their sexual relationship. That positive energy gave fuel to improvements in emotional intimacy.

CONCLUSION

Ken and Helen embraced the vision of cooperatively sharing power. They learned to trust the process and trust each other. Armed with a vision of how to work as a team, the best of each of these two individuals came to the forefront. They stopped being so angry at each other. They learned to talk out their differences.

They showed that, given an opportunity, people will rise to the occasion. But there are limits. We all have our weaknesses. We all have to confront our own competitive, selfish tendencies. I must tell you the truth: To this day, Helen still has a tendency to take control. Ken still has a tendency toward passivity. But they are doing much better.

Part of truly loving someone is learning to accept the imperfections of a partner and learning to roll with the punches. Here is where some of the lessons of the successful sunset couples are so important: We need to have tolerance toward the shortcomings of our partners. We need to respond calmly, with self-discipline, and without letting problems escalate when we are upset with our partners. We need to learn from our experiences and always do better.

When Helen stopped "fixing" Ken, and Ken stopped beating a retreat from his "controlling wife," their marriage improved tremendously. It was interesting that Ken hated Helen's control. But he began remembering how much he loved and admired her high energy. Helen hated Ken's passivity when he didn't do what he said he would do. But she remembered how attracted she had been to his gentle, laid-back spirit. The two of them discovered that couples can share power as equals and love each other without being preoccupied with who is on top and who is on bottom.

CHAPTER 2

Love Story

"He's driving me crazy with the remote control clicker," Janet said to me. "I'll be watching a show, and he'll start changing stations.

"You know," she said, as she calmed herself a little and turned toward her husband, "it really hurts that you do this. It's so selfish. It's so self-centered. You don't care about me, or about my feelings."

"I'm sorry I upset you," Ralph answered, sounding sincere. "It's an old habit."

For just a moment the tension in the room decreased slightly.

Then Ralph again addressed Janet: "You know, you're overreacting. You can't build a good relationship by picking on little things like this."

"Hey," Janet answered with increased annoyance, "it's not a little thing. I told you before that this was important. You said you would stop clicking on me . . . and you haven't."

"Wait a minute," Ralph said, intending to respond.

"No, you wait," Janet said, "I haven't finished talking. You never give a decent apology. You say you're sorry, but then you criticize me for complaining. Can't I tell you that I'm upset about something without you turning it around and saying it's all *my* fault?"

"And"—she paused for a moment, as if to emphasize what followed—"I want to know how you're going to break this habit with the remote control clicker."

"Do I get a turn?" Ralph asked sarcastically.

"Go ahead," Janet answered, almost smiling.

"I'm sorry," Ralph said again. "But I've mostly stopped using the clicker. Are you paying attention? (pause) Haven't you noticed? It's not like I haven't changed."

There was a hint of anger in his voice.

"Hey, are you *really* sorry?" Janet asked, detecting Ralph's annoyance. "Or are you just trying to appease me?"

"I told you I'm sorry. What do you want me to do, beg your forgiveness? You know, you could be apologizing to me for making such a big deal out of something so small."

"You know," Janet replied, "you make me crazy. You really do."

This discussion between Ralph and Janet took place in my office. I listened long enough to see that they were beginning to dig in their heels. It had become a contest to see who would prevail: Could she get him to apologize and stop clicking? Could he silence her complaints?

I knew this couple well. It's not at all evident in this dialogue, but they were two wonderful individuals with a pretty good marriage. Like all couples who had been together for only a relatively short time, they were struggling with inevitable problems. They were making the transition from being individuals, alone on their own, to being individuals who were part of a couple. They had serious communication problems. They also had problems sharing power. In our competitive society, one of the hardest challenges for a couple is *learning how to share power as equals*. We are trained to take power or give it away, but not to share it. As you will see throughout this book, most people lack a vision of cooperation. Even among those who are aware of this option and seek it, most lack the skills to succeed. The result is power struggles and power imbalances that undermine the ability of people to satisfy and make each other happy—which happens to be one of the basic goals of loving relationships.

In some relationships, enormous amounts of energy are wasted by partners who aggressively compete for dominance. As the balance of power shifts back and forth, both individuals usually feel that they are losing. Both feel cheated.

In other relationships, one person assumes the dominant position while the other is submissive. On a short-term basis, this seems to be a perfect match. But in the long run, this inequality creates major problems. The submissive person eventually becomes resentful. The dominant person loses respect for the submissive one.

In contrast, when couples build a cooperative relationship, everybody wins, no one loses. People pool their energy in a synergistic way, producing more benefits together than they could alone. They share the "goodies" and waste none of their energy in competition. There is more for everyone. Everyone feels loved.

Listening to Ralph and Janet's argument about the remote control clicker, you wouldn't know the depth of feelings they had for each other. I was aware of it because I knew their history. They met a year and a half earlier, at one of my relationship workshops. I had been counseling each of them individually. At the workshop, their magnetic attraction was evident to everyone in attendance. Since that time, they had developed an enormous amount of affection for each other.

They were not selfish people. Each wanted to be loved and to give love to a partner. Through their counseling, they recognized the importance of sharing power and had agreed to work together as a team. Much of the time they succeeded in this endeavor. Much of the time they could think clearly about relationships. They understood that a successful relationship meant making each other happy. But when their emotions were aroused and certain types of conflict erupted, they seemed to lose a grip on what they were doing. Their communication broke down. Their competitiveness kicked in: They were slugging it out, fearful that they might be hurt, mistreated, or misunderstood. At these times they became self-centered and couldn't take care of each other.

THE POWER STRUGGLE

Reviewing the dialogue about the remote control clicker, you can see that Janet started by expressing annoyance about Ralph changing stations. That was fine. However, she then tacked on a little editorial about him being selfish, self-centered, and not caring about her feelings. This was provocative because she knew he cared about her. But when she was upset, she lost sight of this and added some sting to her statement—an extra oomph to try to get her way.

Ralph did well to overlook the sting. He responded by saying he was sorry. But he didn't leave it at that. He told her that she complained too much. So, he communicated two messages: One was his concern that he upset her; the other was his complaint that either she shouldn't be upset, or shouldn't say anything about it.

At this point, Janet said that her anger came from the long history they had of arguing about the clicker. Ralph needed to hear this information. But before he had a chance to think about it, Janet added a second complaint: that he didn't give good apologies. She was right, but now she was talking about two things at the same time.

Ralph again said he was sorry, but then accused Janet of trying to "rub his nose in it."

I explained that they were dealing with too many issues at once, and named a few of them: how to live together in a home that has a television with a remote control clicker; how to express feelings; how to listen to a partner without getting defensive; how to negotiate differences; and how to handle apologies.

Most of all, I stressed that their argument had become an issue of mistrusting and doubting each other's love. Janet wondered, "Is he selfish? Does he really care about me? If he did, why would he click while I was watching a show?"

Ralph wondered, "Does she care about my feelings? Is she capable of having a loving relationship? If so, why was she creating a big problem about such a small issue? Why didn't she accept my apology? Why wasn't she more appreciative of me?"

Because the argument about the remote control clicker was intensified enormously by fears about not being loved, I thought it was important to remind them of their underlying, strong affection for each other. *In the heat of arguments, people forget that they care about their partners. They forget that their partners care about them.* They feel alone and vulnerable. They slip into a competitive mode and start thinking that one person will have to prevail over the other. Often they don't realize, or can't keep in mind, that *reasonable and cooperative people who love each other can find solutions to their problems that will satisfy both persons.*

LOVER'S PANIC

As they were discussing the remote control clicker, intense feelings started to stir inside each of them. Ralph was thinking that Janet was too angry and too unforgiving. He began to wonder if he had made a mistake by marrying her. After all, he thought, he had apologized to her for the clicking. For the most part he had stopped clicking—except during commercials. Now she seemed to be making such a big deal out of a little issue. He wondered if she would be capable of building a mature relationship.

Ralph was experiencing what I have named *lover's panic*. This occurs when small problems, or minor incidents, with spouses or dating partners cause people to panic. They fear that they won't be loved, or they'll be consistently hurt, disappointed, or somehow cheated or mistreated in a serious way. They exaggerate the importance of minor problems and overgeneralize the significance of isolated incidents. They get too upset and can't deal with little issues in an appropriate, calm way because they fear that the whole relationship is defective.

Lover's panic undermines confidence about a partner's character and ability to have a high-quality relationship. It prevents commitment. People who suffer from lover's panic either stay single and reject potential mates, or get married but stay aloof because they forever doubt that their relationship will succeed. Both Ralph and Janet had a touch of doubt.

Lover's panic means running scared and should be differentiated from substantial, valid concerns that people might have about their partners and the viability of a relationship.

As we talked about lover's panic in our therapy session, it took us back to their single days. Lover's panic had consistently interfered with Ralph's previous relationships. When he was single, he wanted intimacy and longed for a loving, committed relationship. Time and again he would develop basically good relationships with good women.

Women found him to be warm, fun-loving, successful, and attractive. He appeared to be a real "catch." Women liked that he valued intimacy and was willing to talk openly about his feelings. However, for more than fifteen years he had been moving from one relationship to another.

Like many people who are single for a long time, he wondered if he had been too choosy. But when he thought back about his partners, he had concluded that he made the right decisions. There were certain flaws with each of the women he ultimately rejected.

Before breaking up, he had asked some of the women to work on the problems he identified. For the most part, they did.

Still, the women fell short of his expectations, and the relationships ended. So when Ralph came for therapy, he attributed his single status to chance. He just hadn't met a woman who fit the bill.

Through his therapy, however, Ralph was surprised to discover that his single status was not entirely the result of bad luck. He had been seeking perfection, a relationship in which everything exactly fit his own specifications. If something didn't fit, he took the deviance as evidence that his partner could never properly love him and that a long-term relationship would be impossible. He didn't realize that *all individuals and all relationships have problems and imperfections. Some of the problems can be solved through hard work, but others must be accepted as "part of the package."*

A few of the women Ralph dated wouldn't put up with his perfectionist standards. Others tried with all their heart to make him happy. But no one could ever make Ralph feel the way he wanted to feel—totally secure and guaranteed that his relationship would work the way he wanted it to work. Consequently he left behind a trail of hurt women. Some were confused and felt inadequate. Others were angry and sick of constantly being told that they were wrong and never "good enough."

Through his individual counseling, Ralph began to see that lover's panic had been holding him back. He could not build the "perfect partner." He had been too negative in his thinking. If he wanted to settle down, he would have to find someone who excited him, met many of his needs, and with whom he could work cooperatively to build a relationship. By the time he met Janet, he had made significant progress in overcoming lover's panic, although sometimes, as with the clicker incident, it recurred.

Janet had her own variety of lover's panic that was also stimulated by the remote control argument. In her previous relationships, she had let selfish guys control and dominate her. She had been passive and did not usually say what she was feeling. When she was upset about something, she would quietly withdraw rather than speak out. She never wanted to upset her partners. If they were upset, she generally assumed that she had done something wrong. She would blame herself and almost always accommodate their wishes. As a result, she was often hurt by men who took advantage of her.

Janet had come a long way in individual therapy. She developed greater self-esteem and assertiveness. She stopped blaming herself for everything. She began to express her hurt and angry feelings. She learned to ask for what she wanted.

Janet also decided to approach relationships differently. Because of bad choices in the past, she was very carefully looking for someone who "had it together." She was alarmed when men appeared to be selfish. Ralph seemed fine at first. But at times she would panic: She thought, "Isn't it selfish the way Ralph uses the remote control clicker?"

Janet knew she would no longer accept a submissive position. She didn't want to be hurt and controlled. However, she didn't quite understand the process of two people cooperatively and respectfully resolving problems. In an effort to express her feelings, she sometimes would become too strident or too pushy. This is exactly what she was doing when she was saying, "You don't care about me. You're selfish."

I told Ralph and Janet what I have told many couples for many years: *Conflict is inevitable in relationships. Even the most loving people in the most compatible relationships have conflict. People always have differences. The important issue is how they resolve their differences.* People who love each other can preserve their happiness by learning to work through their differences cooperatively. Instead of panicking when conflict occurs and assuming a relationship is doomed, you first need to make a strong effort to face and solve the problems as a team.

CALMING YOURSELF

Ralph, Janet, and I had discussed cooperative relationships at great length before the argument about the remote control clicker. Both of them wanted to share power. Both wanted an equal relationship. They both knew the importance of working as a team, and realized that competitive attitudes, feelings, and ways of thinking were hard to overcome.

As we talked, I reminded them how hard it is for people to stay on track with cooperation, especially when they get upset and frightened. At these times they fear they'll be hurt or cheated. They feel compelled to put up their dukes, or else become submissive, backing down to avoid conflict at all cost. I could see Ralph and Janet preparing for battle. I reminded them of their affection:

"I've known you both for some time now. I know how much you love each other. But the two of you kind of lose sight of your good feelings when you start to argue. You need to remember your love. Ralph, you know that Janet loves you. Janet, you know that Ralph loves you. Neither of you would deliberately hurt the other. Both of you want the other one to be happy. Think about it as you talk."

This was not a generic pep talk. I couldn't have made the same statement to just any couple. But I knew that Ralph and Janet did love each other and wanted to make each other happy. I knew they had made a serious commitment to cooperate and had already begun to confront their own competitive tendencies. However, these tendencies die slowly. Thus it made sense to remind them of their affectionate feelings and cooperative agreement.

I reminded them that *people in loving, cooperative relationships need to calm themselves down when they start arguing. They need to remember that they are not competing.* It is not a battle to see who wins. They are a team trying to solve problems together. If one person dominates the other, then they have failed.

In the counseling session I suggested some thoughts about partnership, communication, humility, and the cooperative process that people in love relationships should bear in mind when trying to calm themselves down. I urged Ralph and Janet to take note and get in the habit of reminding themselves of these often forgotten thoughts:

Partnership

- You love your partner.
- Your partner loves you.
- You're on the same side. You're working together.

Communication

- People who love each other should communicate in a loving, disciplined, and respectful way.
- It is important to understand and respect each other's thoughts and feelings.
- It is important to hear each other's point of view and to clarify differences.

Humility

- As certain as you may be about the correctness of your own point of view, you still could be wrong or partially wrong. Your partner could be right.
- You both could be right. You both could be wrong.
- You might be misunderstanding your partner.

The Cooperative Process

- There is a cooperative process that allows people to settle their differences with fairness and goodwill.

- You don't have to be scared. You don't have to fight. When cooperating, no one wants to dominate. The goal is to take care of each other.
- People who work as a team and talk calmly, with love, can find solutions to problems that are acceptable to both individuals.

Ralph and Janet needed to get back to the cooperative mode, to believe in each other, and to believe in the process of finding cooperative solutions to problems. If they worked as a team, they surely could settle their differences about the remote control clicker.

To help Ralph and Janet, I provided a model of "self-talk." I suggested they should say something like this to themselves:

"We love each other. We need to calm down and huddle up as a team. We need to find solutions that work for both of us. If we calm down, we will settle our differences and both feel good."

APOLOGIES FROM THE HEART

From previous counseling sessions, Ralph and Janet knew that cooperative couples need to practice calm and disciplined communication, with both parties openly expressing their thoughts and feelings—even negative ones—in loving and nonthreatening ways. They also must listen nondefensively. This is the only way to understand and take care of each other and to talk through their differences.

With encouragement to overcome lover's panic, they were now beginning to calm down. Ralph's communication improved. He admitted he had been defensive when Janet raised the issue of the remote control clicker. He said he thought he had been doing pretty well with the clicker until she complained. Her complaint kind of "deflated" his balloon.

As Janet had indicated earlier, this was not their first argument about the remote control. She had complained before that Ralph would change stations while she was watching a show. Actually, he never changed stations when he *thought* she was watching a show. He would only change when he thought she was doing something else. Janet clarified the misunderstanding by explaining that she would often do two things at once, such as watch television and sew, or watch television and skim through a magazine. Although her undivided attention was not on the television set, she was still watching. Ralph hadn't realized this. When Janet explained, he understood and agreed not to change shows without checking with her first.

Since that discussion, Ralph had almost completely stopped his practice of changing stations during shows. On only a few occasions had he slipped up. However, frequent use of the remote control clicker must have been in his genes—some women argue it's in the Y chromosome—because he continued to change stations during commercial breaks.

In our session, Janet explained that she didn't like Ralph clicking away during commercials because she never knew whether he intended to change back, and sometimes when he did, they missed the beginning of the program that had already resumed.

Ralph said he was sorry he had been so angry and defensive at the start of our session. He hadn't understood Janet's complaint. However, he still maintained that Janet was wrong to say that he was selfish, didn't love her, and didn't care about her happiness. And he especially resented that Janet didn't accept his apologies when they had been talking earlier in our session.

Janet admitted that she had been undisciplined in calling him selfish. She apologized for that. However, she insisted that Ralph's apologies in the beginning of the session had been inadequate. Although he said the words "I'm sorry," Janet did not believe he meant them.

As we talked, it became clear that Ralph didn't fully understand the concept of sincere, cooperative apologies. Such apologies differ completely from formal, insincere apologies, which merely involve uttering the words "I'm sorry" without necessarily caring about the other person's feelings. The words are spoken to be proper and absolve oneself of guilt. After the formality is complete, people making insincere apologies often resume with their own agenda, just as Ralph had. First he said, "I'm sorry," then he started arguing that Janet shouldn't have been complaining in the first place. He really felt that it was *she* who had made the mistakes. That's why Janet never felt better after Ralph said he was sorry. It was as if he had said, "I'm sorry, *but* you shouldn't have complained."

Insincere apologies such as the one Ralph made are often followed by a "but," as in these examples:
- I'm sorry I hurt your feelings, but you hurt mine first.
- I'm sorry for what I did, but it was really your own fault.

In contrast, *cooperative apologies are from the heart. When you have hurt someone you love, you want to take responsibility for the pain and help that person heal.* You say you're sorry with feeling. Because hurt feelings don't always go away immediately, you repeat the apology as much as needed to help the person recover. Touching and other forms of tenderness help.

Ralph's natural inclination would have been to help Janet feel better. But because of his lover's panic and defensiveness, he lost sight of this.

When Ralph finally calmed himself down in our session, he started to feel more tender. As we talked, he realized that his earlier apologies were ineffective and that Janet was not trying to "rub his nose in it," as he had believed. Ralph sincerely felt sorry about his occasional slipups with the remote control clicker. He also was glad that he now knew how Janet felt about him changing stations during commercial breaks. Calmed down and with a better understanding of apologies, he was able to offer a sincere "I'm sorry" undiluted by criticism or counter-complaint.

Janet was slow to bounce back. She worried that Ralph might be a selfish person. She was still somewhat panicky. But Ralph finally seemed to have understood what a cooperative apology entails. He kept repeating that he was sorry. He enhanced his apology by saying that he would work even harder at being careful not to change stations while she was watching a show. He also said he wanted to work with Janet to make a good agreement about how to handle the clicker during commercials. Janet would have preferred if he had offered to stop using it totally. But she recognized that he was offering to talk in a cooperative spirit.

Ralph kept saying he was sorry. He stuck with his apology and asked Janet if there was anything he could do to help her feel better.

Slowly Janet calmed herself down. She was able to relax and recognize that Ralph had no intention of hurting her feelings. He was not being selfish. He was not going back on a previous commitment. At last she could fully accept his apology. Then she was able to say that she was sorry for her part: that she reacted so strongly to this misunderstanding. Janet recognized that the problem could have been resolved much more easily if she had been able to talk about it calmly, without accusations.

RESOLVING THE CLICKER ISSUE

Both Ralph and Janet were reasonable people. I had talked with them at length about cooperative negotiation during previous sessions. They knew that couples need to settle their differences so each person feels satisfied. They knew that right now both of them needed to stop panicking so that the clicker problem could be put in perspective. Ralph's use of the clicker did not mean he was unsuitable for a relationship. Janet's strong reaction did not mean she could not be a loving person. What they needed to do was calm down and find a solution that worked for both of them.

They struggled a little in the negotiation process until Ralph finally proposed a compromise. He said he would click only during commercials, *always* change back to the station they were watching, and *always* tune back before the show resumed.

Janet said she could live with this as long as he was sure to get back to the show they were watching *before* it resumed. If he was tuning back late, she would want the whole practice of clicking to stop. Ralph agreed to her amendment to his proposal.

The dispute was settled.

FIXING THE MOOD

Our session was going well, so we kept talking about the importance of apologies. "When relationships are moving on all eight cylinders," I said, "people apologize quickly." There's no waiting to see who will go first. And it works just as it had with them during this session. Sincere apologies build goodwill. One person shows that he or she cares, and the other reciprocates. Each takes responsibility for his or her share of the problem. It feels good to give a heartfelt apology. It's a loving action.

I explained to Ralph and Janet that *the quickest way to resolve an argument successfully is to make a sincere apology for your own wrongdoing, even if you feel your partner has also done wrong.*

Because the spirit of our talk was positive, and the argument was settled, we started talking about what to do after arguments end. I told them about the concept I call *"cheering up the team."* After settling an argument, it is especially important to repair the mood, for a couple to get close and help each other heal. Both partners should take responsibility for this often overlooked task.

Ralph and Janet responded well to what I was saying. They smiled at each other. Janet reached for Ralph's hand and asked, "Are you feeling okay?"

"I'm fine," he answered. "How about you?"

"I'm okay, too. Let's go out for dinner tonight."

"That sounds great to me."

With this, their work was completed for the day.

ONCE IN A BLUE MOON

Ralph and Janet learned quickly. Their relationship kept improving. I knew that they were doing well when a few weeks later they told me about an argument they had nipped in the bud. This occurred when they were inviting friends to their home for a barbecue and disagreed about whether to serve hamburgers or chicken.

Janet said, "You know I prefer chicken, but we only ever do what I want at barbecues once in a blue moon."

A moment later she realized she was making too big a deal out of this small matter and said with a smile, "Why don't we have hamburgers this time. I don't really care."

Catching the good spirit, Ralph said, "Fine, but any time you think it's your turn, just say, 'It's a blue moon,' and I promise we'll serve what you want at that barbecue."

That was their deal, and they kept it. About half the time, Janet would say, "I think it's a blue moon," and they would serve chicken. Otherwise it was beef. They seemed to have captured the spirit of sharing and compromise. No one wanted to dominate. No one felt cheated. The process was cheerful.

In the ensuing months, Ralph and Janet had lots of fun together and developed lots of goodwill. The cooperativeness was contagious. With all these good feelings, it was relatively easy for them to divide household responsibilities and other tasks without much upset.

HAVING A BABY

When Ralph and Janet stopped coming for counseling, they seemed to have a solid relationship. I thought my work was done.

A year later, I was surprised when they came back in crisis.

Not long after we stopped meeting, Janet discovered she was pregnant. They had planned to start a family, but the baby arrived a couple of years before the projected date.

Janet's pregnancy wasn't an easy one. There was much discomfort and several complications. However, Ralph and she managed to hang together. They took childbirth education classes and looked forward to the excitement of parenthood.

Instead of the joyful natural childbirth they had planned, their baby girl was delivered in an emergency C-section. Fortunately, mother and baby were healthy. Janet, however, was incapacitated for several weeks. During those weeks, Ralph had to pick up the slack. Both of them were sleep-deprived.

The serious problems began over the next several weeks. Janet had a leave of absence from work. Ralph felt the pressure of supporting the now expanding family. For the first time in his life, he became ambitious about earning a hefty income. He worked harder than ever.

At night he wanted to relax after completing all his hard work. On weekends he wanted to play, just as the two of them had played before the baby was born. But he couldn't get Janet to participate in the old type of fun. He resented this and complained. Janet felt guilty and apologized for being a "party pooper." She felt she should play, too. At the same time, she also thought that the play was frivolous and that she and Ralph needed to be facing their duties as parents. Furthermore, she needed help.

As good as the relationship had been to this point, both found themselves under enormous stress: Ralph as a provider, and Janet as the parent predominantly responsible for child care. Ralph didn't understand the impact of parenthood and wasn't supportive enough with practical help in caring for the baby. Janet reverted to her old practice from previous relationships of holding in her feelings. She couldn't ask for help and couldn't communicate the extent of her exhaustion and need. Once again, she panicked that she might have married a selfish man. Ralph detected Janet's resentment and panicked that he might have picked an angry, unloving woman. He accused Janet of neglecting the marriage for the sake of the baby. Worse still, both felt trapped—married and with a child.

Ralph and Janet knew something was wrong, and quickly came for counseling. Overwhelmed by pressure and demands, each had blamed the other for the burdens. Each accused the other of not sharing the weight of the new responsibilities. It had happened: They slipped back into the competitive mode. They started seeing each other as antagonists, not partners.

I explained that they were misinterpreting their problem. Neither was to blame for the enormous burden each felt. That burden is what all couples experience with the birth of a child. When a baby is born, people must learn new roles, including the role of being a parent. They have less time for fun and more economic pressure. Both are sleep-deprived. It can be enormously stressful.

Because our society is not particularly supportive of children and families, the burden crashes down heavily. Under this burden, many people start to blame each other, just as Ralph and Janet had done.

I reassured them that neither person had been slacking off. I explained that they needed to work together because this would probably be one of the hardest working epochs of their lives. It was no time to panic. Instead Ralph needed to help more with the baby, and perhaps pace himself better on his job. Janet had to start talking about her feelings instead of quietly holding them back. Both needed to express appreciation for each other's efforts and hard work. They needed to find new outlets for fun within the constraints of being the parents of an infant daughter. Most of all, they should celebrate their baby and strive to do more to help each other.

All Ralph and Janet needed was a reminder about working as a team and a little pep talk. They pulled it together again.

But here they were: two good people with lots of love. They understood the horrendous effects of competition on loving relationships. They had worked hard to build a cooperative feeling between themselves. But even this couple—with their basically positive start—slipped back into the competitive mode. That's how hard it is to overcome competition.

TOLERANCE

As I write this chapter, Ralph and Janet have been together for more than eight years. They now are a happy, successful couple with two daughters.

I got confirmation of their success not too long ago, when Ralph came to see me to discuss his feelings about his father's health problems. At the time, Ralph told me how well Janet and he were doing. He even described an incident that had occurred recently. Janet was upset after a tough day. Ralph suggested that she drink a glass of wine to relax. Janet thought he was soft-pedaling her feelings and got upset with him.

"What's with the wine?" she asked. "Are you telling me to take two pills and call you in the morning?"

Ralph knew that he was trying to be supportive and that Janet had misinterpreted what he meant.

"Guess what?" he asked me. "I didn't try to win points about her being so grouchy and out of sorts. I was sorry I had upset her. I hate to see her upset. I told her so, and also asked if I could do anything to cheer her up.

"She just said she needed a little time to snap out of it. So I backed off. She calmed down, and we had a great day. You know what? Sincere apologies work wonders. You taught us that a long time ago."

"No more panic?" I asked.

"No," he said. *"I picked the right person.* Janet's occasional moodiness is a small price to pay for all the great stuff. I love her. She loves me."

It was clear that Ralph and Janet were taking good care of each other and that Ralph had developed a wonderful tolerance and flexibility.

As you can see, even well-intentioned, nice people such as Ralph and Janet had to work hard to build a successful relationship. All people who enter relationships face the challenge of learning to live as a couple. Everyone who is successful has to overcome competitive training and master the ability to share power as equals.

Some of the love stories that follow involve severely distressed couples and do not end as successfully as this one. I believe you can learn as much from the frustrations and failures as from the successes of couples.

CHAPTER

3

The Cooperative Vision

A young man in his early thirties told me about himself, his wife, and his marriage. His relationship started with great "chemistry" that continued during an exciting, intense courtship and through a honeymoon period. But now, five years later, Richard was increasingly disenchanted. He and his wife, Marsha, still had fun when they weren't fighting like cats and dogs, but those times were less and less frequent. At the moment he was fed up with her disapproving attitude and constant nagging. In fact, he came prepared with a written list of complaints to our meeting, his first therapy session.

Item number one was that Marsha didn't appreciate his accomplishments. Although he had been highly successful in his job as a financial adviser, providing a much better standard of living than either of them had ever expected, his wife complained that he didn't earn enough money.

Second, she whined too much. When he would return home at the end of the workday, she wouldn't give him a minute of peace. She was too demanding. "She follows me around the house like a hurt puppy."

Third, she consistently griped about his drinking, even though he would only have a single beer after work and an occasional glass of wine with dinner. Recently Marsha had accused him of being an alcoholic.

Fourth, Marsha didn't carry her share of the workload. By their agreement, she didn't work outside the home. However, she often didn't do the work that she said she would do, such as preparing dinner on weekdays.

What finally led Richard to seek help from me was an argument that occurred the day before he called, during which Marsha proclaimed that dinner wasn't ready because she was "too upset." Richard was tired of that excuse. He told her that he goes to work and carries his load, even when he is upset, and that she should do the same. That particular incident, he said, put him over the brink and into my office.

This, then, was the essence of the gripe list that Richard read to me and embellished with details.

As I listened, I started to wonder about his wife's point of view. Surely Marsha wouldn't say, "I'm the cause of all our marital problems. I'm unappreciative of my husband's hard work. I whine too much. I unfairly accuse him of being an alcoholic. I don't carry a fair share of the workload. Fix me, and the relationship will be perfect." There had to be another side to this story.

So I asked Richard why his wife hadn't come to the session. He said that she refused to come because she thought the marital problems were all his fault. He was the one who needed help.

How interesting. He defined the problem by complaining about her. She apparently blamed him. It was a stalemate.

This is not unusual: Most people feel some sort of dissatisfaction and discover problems in their relationship, just as Richard and Marsha had. In searching for an explanation, they find faults, real or imagined, in their partners. Usually each person hopes to change the other one.

They sometimes self-righteously gripe about the other person's wrongdoing. Often they unleash harsh, judgmental criticism. But they also find themselves in a passive position: *waiting for someone else to change.*

Their partners don't budge. People don't usually change themselves, or what they're doing, in response to one-sided criticism. Such criticism usually promotes defensiveness more than anything else. At best, people will make temporary changes or adjustments in response to pressure from their partners. But they resent the pressure. They lack the internal commitment needed to sustain change.

Unfortunately, many people get stuck in this position—each blaming the other—just as Richard and Marsha had.

In general, people are much more willing to admit their own shortcomings when the criticism they receive is balanced and fair. In fact, *the best way to get your partner to admit to problems is to be willing to admit to your own.*

If you want to solve relationship problems, the starting point is to get a balanced picture of what is wrong, which means identifying both your own and your partner's responsibility. Then you can begin to work on yourself, which is the only part of the problem you can control. This usually inspires partners to see and work on their share of the problem. It also puts you in a good position to make constructive criticism and to challenge a partner to grow, even a resistant one.

One person cannot improve a relationship alone. But you don't have to be stuck waiting for a partner to change. One person can provide leadership to start the process. Most relationships can be improved significantly if (1) you are self-critical and (2) you approach a partner constructively.

If your partner doesn't match your effort in working on his part of the problem, you still gain something. You will benefit from your own personal growth. Even with the worst outcome, if the relationship fails to improve because your partner won't budge, you have a choice: You can stay and accept a bad situation, or leave with your head held high, either way knowing that you were self-critical and did everything you could. If you leave, you will be better prepared for future relationships.

A COMPETITIVE STRUGGLE

It took some time, but I was finally able to piece together the whole story of Richard and Marsha's relationship by asking tough questions and by eventually getting the two of them at joint sessions.

As you would expect, when they both told the story, the complete picture was more complex than the way Richard described it from his viewpoint. This is what had happened the day of the argument that led Richard to call for an appointment. In many ways that day was typical of their interaction.

On that day, Richard was driving home, thinking that he needed half an hour alone to relax after a stressful meeting in his office. At that very moment, Marsha eagerly awaited his return, thinking that she wanted adult company after caring for their toddler alone at home all day. Their son was taking a nap.

Marsha greeted Richard at the door and leaned toward him for a kiss. Richard gave a perfunctory little peck and made a sharp cut around her, like an all-star football player. Then he turned and headed toward the refrigerator in search of a beer, Marsha in pursuit.

"Are you my shadow?" he asked with a sarcastic smile and a definite trace of irritation.

"No," she answered, "just a loving wife looking for a little affection from a cold husband."

"Like a hurt puppy," he added, popping off the top of a beer. (This was one of his criticisms of her: "She follows me around like a hurt puppy.")

"Why do you go straight to the refrigerator when you come home?" she asked. "It seems like you're using alcohol as a crutch or something. I think you've got a drinking problem." (This was another of Richard's criticisms: her unfair accusations about alcoholism.)

Even as she said this, Marsha worried that her words were too strong. But she was hurt. On days like today, he seemed to prefer alcohol over her company. That drink seemed so important to him.

Marsha's comments were enough to inspire another athletic maneuver by Richard, and his retreat into the den with a beer.

Marsha went to the bedroom to cry.

When Richard resurfaced half an hour later, *of course* dinner wasn't ready. Marsha had been in the bedroom, crying.

Richard complained that she wasn't carrying her share of the work around the house (which was another item on his gripe list at his therapy session). Marsha defended herself by saying that he had upset her and that's why dinner wasn't ready.

He called her "irresponsible" and said she was making excuses. She retaliated by saying that he should earn more money so they could afford a cook. It wasn't that she was really dissatisfied with their income, but she was firing back an insult. (Here was his gripe that she complained about their standard of living.) Anyway, Marsha added, it hadn't been her choice to quit her job. He was the one who wanted her to stay home with the baby.

Richard and Marsha didn't know how to resolve conflict. They were engaged in a spiraling, downhill, *competitive* battle for dominance, each fighting for himself or herself. Both of them felt oppressed and cheated. Both were dissatisfied. Neither was happy. Neither felt appreciated. And they repeated this same argument and discussion, with only minor variations, almost every day. They were in an attack/counterattack mode.

Competitive behavior such as this is a serious impediment to loving relationships. Many couples compete, just as Richard and Marsha did, for the upper hand. They start this pattern without even realizing it, driven by unconscious conditioning about how to handle differences and by deep-rooted fears of being cheated or unloved. They are in the on-guard, "dukes up" position. They think that the only way to get what they want is selfishly to fight for their own self-interest. In fact, they are confused: To create loving relationships, individuals must overcome these competitive tendencies.

It was a sad and frustrating state of affairs for Richard and Marsha. They had started their relationship with great love and excitement. Now they were tearing each other apart. If the battle continued on the current course, anger would eventually overshadow and diminish the positive feelings. Wisely they had chosen to come for help in time. Many couples wait much too long, until the bitterness is intense and the romantic juices have dried. At that point the chance of repairing the relationship is slim.

Once the full picture of what was happening in this "after-work dispute" between Marsha and Richard became evident, three main issues emerged:

1. How to handle the first few minutes at the end of the day. Richard wanted a chance to decompress, and Marsha wanted affection and attention.
2. How to establish and clarify shared goals (about income, work outside the home, and lifestyle).
3. How to divide responsibilities for child care and work around the house.

These are typical problems that confront many couples. Couples often have conflicting needs at the end of the workday. They also frequently disagree about the division of labor in a household, careers, finances, and personal values related to raising children. All these problems are intensified during times of family stress. In this case, Richard and Marsha had a toddler at home.

The fact that this couple had conflict was nothing extraordinary. Conflict about big and small matters is inevitable in all relationships. Any two people—even those who are highly compatible and wonderfully cooperative—will always have disagreements about day-to-day matters, such as which restaurant to pick for dinner or what movie to rent, and about basic value issues such as how to raise children and how to budget family income. *Given that conflict is inevitable, the key to a successful relationship is how the differences are expressed and resolved.* The overriding problem with Marsha and Richard was that they didn't know how to communicate respectfully or how to resolve conflict. Therefore they could not work out cooperative and loving solutions to their differences.

LOCKED HORNS

The most serious problems in love relationships almost always involve one person doing something that reinforces a behavior that he or she dislikes in a partner, creating a vicious circle. I call this interaction *locking horns*.

Richard wanted quiet time alone at home. Yet by ignoring Marsha when he returned from work, he hurt her. The more hurt she felt, the more she pressed for his attention, and the less chance Richard had for gaining quiet time.

Marsha wanted Richard's attention. The more aggressively she pursued it, the greater was Richard's urge to withdraw. The more he withdrew, the more neglected she felt.

Their problems were escalating into an inescapable pattern. She couldn't stand his withdrawal. He couldn't put up with her demands for attention. Yet unwittingly, both did something that encouraged what each most disliked in the other.

The solution was a paradox: To attain solitude, Richard needed to give Marsha attention. To get attention, Marsha needed to give Richard solitude.

A COOPERATIVE VISION

I explained to Richard and Marsha that their "me first" attitude would never work, because if one person dominated, the other was going to resent it. Furthermore, neither effectively managed to gain the upper hand. Both were dissatisfied.

I helped them realize that their arguments were costly. Both felt as if they were losing. Both felt that the other one was better off. In fact, neither was doing well.

Then I explained something that seems obvious when you think about it but tends to be forgotten in our highly competitive society: *The essence of a loving relationship is that two people make each other happy.* A relationship is not successful if only one person feels good or, in this case, if no one feels good. When conflict arises, a couple has to find cooperative solutions that satisfy both individuals. I suggested to Richard and Marsha that they change their attitude from "me against him (or her)" to "let's be a team and take care of both of us." Instead of fighting to see which would prevail after work, they should be looking to find a solution that would satisfy both of them.

Many people find it difficult to see the value of cooperation. We are conditioned to think that competition brings out the best in us. We equate success with victory—that is, with beating someone else. This win-lose logic is called zero-sum thinking, so named because one person's gain is canceled by another's loss. When you add the benefits and losses, there is no overall gain. Those who use zero-sum thinking don't see that in many situations, especially in a family, both sides would gain by cooperating.

Like any couple who want a loving relationship, Richard and Marsha first needed a *cooperative vision* of a husband and wife working as a team, on the same side, trying to meet each other's needs.

They needed to understand that cooperation results in more for everyone; each would be better off. As a team, the whole becomes greater than the sum of the parts. Most important, the spirit of cooperation preserves the good, loving feelings they have for each other. With a cooperative vision guiding their action, Richard and Marsha could stop wasting energy in a competitive struggle for dominance.

BASIC COOPERATIVE AGREEMENT AND COOPERATIVE SKILLS

A good starting point for people who want a loving, cooperative relationship is to make an agreement to work as a team to meet each other's needs. A formal arrangement of this sort is called a Basic Cooperative Agreement (BCA). With a BCA, the two individuals strive for equality. They agree that no one tries to dominate, and no one takes a subordinate position. They pool their energy so the whole is greater than the sum of the parts. In that way there is more for everyone.

When I explained a BCA, Richard said that Marsha is "too concerned about herself to even think about cooperating."

"Yeah," she replied, "in here you'll say that you want to cooperate so you'll look good with Dr. Schwebel, but when we get home, you'll only think about yourself."

Both took several more potshots before they began to recognize their pattern: They were competing over a cooperative agreement. Each thought that the other was untrustworthy. After much discussion they could see the necessity of changing their attitudes, and began to budge. It took several sessions, but they finally understood the importance of finding cooperative solutions to their conflict so *both* could be satisfied and so their good feelings for each other could be preserved and expanded again.

I explained that when they argued, one of them needed to be what my mother used to call the "big boy." (She used that expression when my brother and I argued as children.) The big boy is the one who stops blaming the other person and starts the process of resolving the conflict. Either Richard or Marsha needed to say, "We have a problem. We have conflict. We must find a solution that works for both of us."

Their "afterwork problem" should be redefined. They should ask themselves: How can we find a solution to our problems at 5:00 P.M. so that both of us feel okay?

The solution shouldn't be exactly the way either of them wants it to be. Rather, there should be some middle ground that would satisfy both of them.

Even when couples understand the benefits of cooperation, they still find it difficult to put their beliefs into practice. In part this is because of our enormous conditioning to compete. Our economic survival and prosperity on a day-to-day basis depend on working in a competitive—sometimes intensely competitive—environment. It is difficult to be tense and aggressive for eight hours each day at the workplace and then to return home and become a calm, gentle, and sensitive person. But to build a loving relationship, people must transcend both a lifetime of competitive conditioning and the daily reinforcement of competitive behavior.

Another reason why it is difficult to put cooperative values into practice is that people lack cooperative skills, such as the ability to see the other person's perspective, to communicate cooperatively, and to negotiate. But the good news is that people with a cooperative vision and the will to cooperate can master these skills. You will see that it is possible in this and other love stories in this book.

COOPERATION AND NEGOTIATION

As I walked Richard and Marsha through the cooperative process, they were able to find practical solutions to all of their major problems in the following several weeks. The beginning point was to learn *perspective-taking*—that is, *the ability to see things from a partner's point of view.*

We dubbed the afterwork issue the "five-o'clock battle."

"Marsha won't give me a moment to relax when I come home," Richard had complained. "She follows me like a hurt puppy."

"That's because," Marsha had answered, "you can be as cold as ice. You need to thaw out."

Through perspective-taking in the session, Richard gradually recognized that his wife had been home alone with the baby all day, that she approached him for a kiss, and that she was hurt by his lack of interest.

Marsha began to understand that Richard was tired and wanted some solitude to recover from the day's work in the office.

Once they began to see that each opposing point of view had some validity, we began to talk about negotiation. I explained that there are basically three ways to resolve conflict cooperatively. One is through *compromise*, in which you meet each other halfway. Another is by *trade-off*: Your way this time, my way next time. The third approach is *creative solutions*. This one means discovering an alternative that fully satisfies each person. I explained that people give up on seeking creative solutions much too soon. With all our competitive training, we're not really good at inventing options that make both people happy. But often they exist. I like to give the example of a husband and wife who argued about where to go on a vacation. He wanted to go to the mountains. She wanted a seaside resort. After much bickering they suddenly realized that they could go to the northern California coast, where the mountains meet the ocean. It was a creative solution that satisfied both of them.

It was relatively easy for Richard and Marsha to negotiate a cooperative solution to the five-o'clock battle. They agreed to a compromise of starting the evening with a warm greeting at the door followed by five minutes together when Richard first returned from work. But then Richard was free to retreat and relax, undisturbed for half an hour. He was comfortable with the warm greeting and five-minute interaction, knowing that shortly he would have time alone. Marsha was comfortable with his taking time alone, knowing that it would be preceded by a warm greeting and followed by more time together.

They chose this approach after discussing and rejecting two other possibilities. One was a shorter initial greeting—just a warm kiss followed by time apart. The other was to take turns. One day they would be together after work, the next day apart.

Finding a cooperative solution to the five-o'clock battle was a real boost for their relationship. It had been a long-standing argument. They could see that they were not "selfish people" but that their conflict was caused by a lack of cooperative vision and skills. Now they were beginning to learn perspective-taking and negotiation.

As they put their agreement into practice and continued to negotiate other differences cooperatively, they began to feel better about each other and to gain increasing awareness of the other person's needs. One of Richard's reactions when they put the plan into action was that he was no longer so eager to *avoid* Marsha. He felt more that they were a team, and therefore he had less desire to escape from her presence. He even began to see her as a potential source of support. As Marsha felt Richard's increased concern for her feelings, she had less need to command his attention. She knew she could count on good times together, even if she stopped pushing for them.

THE SUPER DECISION

At Richard and Marsha's first session together I had introduced them to a concept that I call the super decision, which is the emotional counterpart to the Basic Cooperative Agreement. The super decision is no abstraction to me. I developed the idea from personal experience about twenty years ago. At that time I was engaged in some sort of argument with my parents, who, I should say, happen to be wonderful and understanding people. I don't remember the specifics of the dispute, but I do recall that I wasn't proud of my own behavior. I felt I was upsetting them unnecessarily and acting in an emotionally careless way.

It was interesting how things evolved. I was unhappy with my behavior and wanted to change. I was able to change by thinking ahead to the time when my parents would be very old. Thinking to the future, I had a strong feeling that I didn't want them to look back at our relationship and be disappointed. Rather, I wanted to enrich their lives—be wonderful to them just as they had been to me. I wanted them to be filled with good feelings about me, just as I had been filled with good feelings for them. I also wanted to feel proud of myself. So twenty years ago I made what I recently started calling the *super decision*—that is, *I committed myself to a high standard of behavior with the people I loved*. To maintain a high standard of behavior, I knew I would need self-discipline. I would have to monitor myself closely to make sure that I didn't impulsively or callously hurt my parents. I wanted to avoid unnecessary pain. I knew that at times I would have strong feelings I would want to express, but I committed myself to thinking before I acted, and to communicating in a careful and disciplined way.

I soon discovered that following through with the super decision also required an equal commitment to the development of cooperative communication skills. I had to find positive and constructive ways to communicate my thoughts and feelings.

The super decision significantly improved my relationship with my parents. In a way, I recognized that I had control over my own destiny in a relationship. I could write my own history. I can't say that there haven't been times that I wish I had done better, but the decision has served as an important reminder to watch myself and to use serious self-control when my emotions are aroused. As you know, emotions are often aroused in relationships with parents and other people we love.

Later, when I married my wife, I made the same super decision to behave responsibly. I knew there had been times in previous romantic relationships when I had made hurtful mistakes, when, for example, I had been too quick to make a negative interpretation of something that was said.

The super decision doesn't mean that I don't have conflict. Rather, it means that I'm *careful* in how I deal with my feelings, that I remind myself always to treat the people I love with the love I feel for them. It gives me a sense of control over my history and a bigger view of my relationship, extending far past the immediate moment.

In their therapy session, I urged Richard and Marsha to stop blaming each other and to stop concentrating on the other person's faults. I told them that they both had room for improvement in their own behavior. I said there's no magic in behaving well. We don't become better people just by wishing it. I recommended that they make the super decision and warned that it requires commitment and continuing effort. But, I said, it is the backbone of a cooperative relationship. I told them that they would feel good about themselves as individuals if they stuck to the super decision, regardless of what would happen between them. Both accepted the challenge. Although they had their ups and downs as the months passed, they agreed that the super decision helped them move in the right direction.

CONCLUSION

At Richard and Marsha's third counseling session, I explained to them that resolving the conflict over lifestyle and the division of labor was not as simple as settling the five-o'clock battle. Richard and Marsha needed to have a long series of talks to discuss their values about income, child-care responsibilities, and standard of living. They had to reach an understanding about who would work outside the home. They also had to determine which jobs needed to be done in the home and how that work would be divided. They recognized that their solutions had to satisfy both of them.

In the course of these discussions, they worked hard at *really* listening to each other. They worked at improving their ability in perspective-taking. They clarified misunderstandings. Each made concessions.

Marsha admitted that her "complaint" about Richard not earning more money was simply a fighting tactic, a hurtful comment said in anger. As they discussed Marsha's return to the workforce, both felt it would be premature at this time because of the baby. But Marsha did say she missed the stimulation of work, and needed more recreational activities to compensate. So they started to rent movies on weekdays and planned little outings each weekend. They socialized with friends much more often. Richard became increasingly involved with his role as a parent and carried more responsibility for work around the house. He especially participated in child-care responsibilities during the weekends. Most important, Richard and Marsha felt more like a team after these lengthy discussions. The two of them remembered their loving feelings, and the romantic flames reignited.

They found that people who love each other need to work as a team at all times if they want a happy relationship. And they learned it could be done.

Richard and Marsha discovered that competing for dominance damages a loving relationship. In the next love story, you will see what happens when one partner, rather than competing, becomes completely subordinate to the other. You will see an entirely different set of serious problems.

CHAPTER

4

Dominance and Submission

It started as an ordinary Tuesday morning at work, with Sharon talking for about an hour with the local sales representatives that she managed at a computer software company. Her excitement surged momentarily when her own supervisor informed her that the "big boss" from national headquarters was in town. He wanted to talk with her about the possibility of a major promotion to the position of regional sales manager.

Then her spirits tumbled when her supervisor instructed her to clear her schedule for an eleven-o'clock meeting the following day. Sharon asked if the meeting could be moved up to nine o'clock or back to one o'clock. He said it couldn't, and asked if she had a problem. "No," she answered somewhat hesitantly. But she knew that she had promised to take her boyfriend, Arthur, to the airport for an eleven-thirty flight. She didn't want to disappoint him.

She and Arthur had been dating steadily for about a year and a half. Their relationship fluctuated between stable and rocky on a day-by-day basis, but Sharon loved him and wanted to get married or, at least, live together. In contrast, he was hesitant about committing. Nevertheless, they spent almost every evening and most weekends with each other.

As soon as her boss left the room, Sharon gathered her thoughts and nervously dialed Arthur's phone number. She hoped he would understand the situation but wasn't certain he would.

As she started to explain the job opportunity, Arthur interrupted: "I know what you're going to say. You're going to tell me that you can't take me to the airport tomorrow. Well, that makes me mad."

Then he listed five reasons why she *should* be taking him:
1. He never failed to take her when she needed rides.
2. He had asked for the ride a long time ago. He had turned down other offers.
3. When people are involved in a serious relationship, rides to the airport are one of the "basics."
4. It was a last-minute change; she knew that he hated them.
5. This was yet another example of her failure to come through when needed. (He then listed four previous failures.)

I like to tell this love story to audiences at lectures and workshops. Then I ask the audience what they think Sharon felt, and also what she should do. I've found it interesting that most people think she felt angry and that the most prevalent recommendation is to "dump" the guy because he's too self-centered.

Next I ask the audience what they think Sharon actually did. Almost everyone thinks that she went to the meeting at the designated time, even though I hint at a different outcome by talking about her nervousness in calling Arthur and her desire to please him. Then I tell what really happened: Sharon took Arthur to the airport, just as originally planned.

This is a classic example of the inability of a couple to cooperate. The problem started with a *power play*—that is, one person's attempt to coerce or manipulate another person to do what he or she wanted. In this case Arthur used what could be categorized as a "reasonable"-type power play. Even though we tend to think of force or a threat of some sort when we discuss power plays, many of them, such as this one, are more subtle and manipulative.

In the phone conversation, Arthur interrupted Sharon in midsentence and basically outtalked her. He used his intelligence to argue his point and win an argument, rather than to settle a difference cooperatively. He wanted to get his way and was unconcerned with Sharon's best interest.

All arguments involve two or more people with differing points of view. Any person of average intelligence can easily construct and articulate a rational defense of his or her own viewpoint. In this case, Arthur aggressively argued for his own self-interest. At the same time, he failed to consider Sharon's point of view.

ONE-UP/ONE-DOWN COMPETITION

The shocking part of this scene I described is that Arthur hadn't a clue that he did anything wrong. He thought he was rightfully sticking up for himself. He was so absorbed in his own needs that he never realized that he was completely ignoring Sharon's important career opportunity. Nor did he realize that he panicked as Sharon spoke, worrying that he might have chosen "the wrong woman" who couldn't care about his needs. In the phone conversation, he filtered his perceptions of what was happening through a lens of fear. Because he interrupted her, he never got a chance to find out what she was thinking and planning to say, which, by the way, respected his needs.

First, she never planned unilaterally to withdraw her offer of a ride to the airport. She wanted to discuss the matter. Second, she had several ideas about resolving the problem, including to take him to the airport early, to find someone else who could take him, or to pay for a taxi herself. But Arthur and Sharon never had a give-and-take discussion. Sharon never got to make her proposal.

The sudden impact of Arthur's argument overwhelmed her. First, she felt bad about herself: "I'm so selfish to have raised the issue of the ride at the last minute. After all, I made a promise. I should deliver on it." A few hours later, she was agitated, and her thoughts drifted slightly: "Why is he always right and I'm always wrong?" she wondered. But as hard as she tried, she couldn't answer this question. She just felt bad about herself for being so selfish.

After Arthur convinced her to stick to the original plans, Sharon had to face her supervisor. She explained to him that she couldn't make the eleven-o'clock meeting because of family obligations. He agreed to change the time. Later Sharon felt that this wrinkle in the plans may have been what cost her the promotion: She did not get the new job.

In the next few days, Sharon felt some resentment toward Arthur but didn't feel justified. Although she tried to hide her feelings, they surfaced indirectly through inappropriate, sarcastic remarks. These remarks then served as fodder for what turned out to be Arthur's self-fulfilling prophecy that he might have chosen a woman who didn't care about his feelings.

Sharon was unaware of Arthur's power play, just as Arthur himself had been. She thought that Arthur was reasonable. After all, he gave "good reasons" why she should take him to the airport. She didn't realize that he had verbally overpowered her. She didn't realize that he had negated her feelings by acting as if they were unimportant.

What you have, then, is a couple who could not cooperatively coordinate their efforts to meet all the needs of the two individuals. Without knowing it, they reached a *competitive* solution to their conflict. One person won. The other lost.

As you see, competition is not always two people openly fighting for dominance. Sometimes competition involves one person willingly accepting the submissive position. Some people are trained to win in competition and others to lose, or at least to negotiate from a one-down or inferior position. Arthur clearly learned to compete to win, in this case by using one-sided reasoning.

Sharon had learned that she should take care of other people first, and that asserting her own needs would make her "selfish." She accepted a submissive position. Like Sharon, many people confuse assertiveness (sticking up for themselves) with selfishness (ignoring the needs of others). Consequently they can't assert themselves without guilt. When they think about asserting themselves, they feel they shouldn't. They are vulnerable to power plays—such as Arthur's—that imply they would be selfish to stick up for themselves.

Although not evident to this couple, the detrimental effects of Arthur's abuse of power are clear to most observers. And to most observers Sharon appears to be the innocent victim. Her complicity in their arrangement—the inability to assert herself—is less obvious. Nevertheless, it is equally detrimental to a cooperative relationship. Arthur and Sharon played complementary roles. He put himself first. She conceded his dominance. He implied that she was selfish and that his needs were more important. She *agreed, colluded, and complied* with his program. They were wired for competition. Together they created a win-lose situation. Because they often interacted this way, they had an unequal balance of power in their relationship, a dynamic that always leads to trouble. Sharon eventually resented the unfairness of it all.

RESCUING BEHAVIOR

The subservient attitude is quite prevalent in women because of sex-role conditioning. Girls are trained to think that love means always pleasing the other person. As children, they are told that boys and men will eventually take care of them if they are "nice" and "loving" and willing to put aside their own needs. They are told that sticking up for themselves is selfish. This prepares young females for a position of dependence in relationships. Historically it was an understandable adaptation to a world in which men dominated the workforce. Women were more or less excluded and therefore needed to please men, or win their favor, for their own survival. Nowadays women still earn substantially less in the workplace, and to a certain extent experience similar pressures toward dependence.

Some boys also get training in subservience. Culturally it can be traced, in part, to the shopkeeper mentality: The customer is always right. In other words, if you please others, you will prosper.

Boy and girl "pleasers" are all-giving. They'll do anything for you. They'll do your share of the housework. They'll go where you want to go on vacation. They'll go to the movies you select. Because they won't "burden" others with their feelings, they'll never tell you when they're hurt or angry. ("People who love each other don't get angry.") Because they "save" you from dealing with their needs, they are called "rescuers."

Rescuers try to avoid conflict. They hold back their feelings and let problems fester unresolved. Eventually, however, their hurt and resentment surface. Whatever the sex of the person, whatever the cultural or family roots of the training, this type of subordinate behavior of putting other people first is a major impediment to cooperation.

THE BIG SURPRISE

People may tolerate a subservient position for weeks, months, years, and sometimes decades before getting tired of it. At first they are highly self-critical, just as Sharon was during her conflict with Arthur about a ride to the airport. They think, "My relationship would be better if I were more loving" (or more giving or sensitive or perfect). Many rescuers have an ever-hopeful attitude that improvement is imminent if only they could do better. "If only I could learn to be more loving," they think, "then my partner would love me." Rescuers blame themselves for everything. Often their partners agree. Sharon thought that her own selfishness was keeping Arthur from making a commitment. She was critical of herself and hoped that if she could do better, he would commit to the relationship. Arthur reinforced this belief by his frequent criticism of her "selfishness."

Nothing changes for the better in these one-up/one-down relationships. The emotional time bomb relentlessly ticks. In some cases the anger is turned inward and the subservient person becomes depressed and filled with self-hatred. In the classic example, a subservient woman is highly medicated with antidepressants, or self-medicates with alcohol. In the worst cases, she may attempt suicide. Eventually most subservient people recognize that they are not entirely to blame for what is happening. They see that their partner is dominant. They resent the lack of reciprocation. But at first they may hesitate to act: "I've given so much. I've invested so much. I can't stop now."

Next, they express dissatisfaction. They tell their partners of their unhappiness. Some of them ask that they go together for couples counseling. Usually they find that their concerns are discounted by their partner: "If you're not happy with the relationship, then you should go for help yourself. It's not my problem. I'm satisfied."

Some of the emotional pressure from subservience may be released gradually through sarcasm or unexplainable outbursts over minor incidents. Sooner or later, however, the hurt and resentment grow to crisis proportions.

In desperation, the now very angry person who has been a second-class citizen in the relationship sometimes resorts to dramatic actions, such as having an affair, threatening to file for a divorce, or actually filing for one. The power balance swings in the other direction.

At this point, his or her partner is flabbergasted. Because the angry and hurt feelings were hidden, they didn't see it coming.

I call this pattern of suppressed anger that eventually erupts the *Big Surprise*. But if you understand the underlying dynamics, you realize it isn't at all surprising. People who don't assert their needs and don't do anything about situations that feel bad are likely to become dissatisfied in a major way. It's just a matter of time.

Faced with intense anger and possibly the threat of divorce, some of the partners who before refused to enter marriage therapy are now willing to go. They'll cooperate. They don't want to lose a good thing, although sadly, in many cases, they already have lost it. Often by this time their spouses have an unforgiving explosion of anger: They ask, "Where were you when I was in such pain? How could you take from me for so long without giving back?"

At this point, no matter what the other person does, it may be too late. The anger won't go away.

CODEPENDENCE

One of the most fashionable adjectives to describe people, especially women, in troubled relationships is "codependent." The concept was created when the spouses of alcohol- and drug-dependent people sought the support of peers in similar situations. In their discussions, they began to see patterns in their own behavior, unhealthy ways in which they were coping with drug abuse in their families. They concluded: The person with a drug problem had a chemical dependence. The person in a relationship with him (or her) was codependent.

The codependents found that they were rescuers who tended to give away their power by subordinating their needs to their demanding and troubled partners. They found that they excused misbehavior they attributed to the influence of drugs. Many of them realized that they were scared of doing otherwise. They feared that they would lose their relationships if they were to assert themselves. Sometimes they tried to rescue their troubled partners in another way, by "fixing" or repairing" them. Their motivation was partly to help, and partly self-serving because the drug problem affected them directly.

In their helping efforts, they sometimes took strong positions, such as "no drinking allowed in the house," and strong actions, such as hiding drugs. This resulted in a seesaw power struggle in the families. The codependents alternated between a one-up position of helper/rescuer and a one-down position of victim.

Codependents didn't blame everything on their drug-dependent partners. They saw their own irrational patterns. When a relationship would end with one drug-dependent person, many of them soon found themselves in a relationship with another troubled individual. They seemed to have a need for these unhealthful interactions. They found comfort in helping. It made them feel worthwhile and valuable. Many of them realized that they felt they didn't deserve anything better. It was familiar and comfortable to be "chasing love," trying to win affection from a self-centered partner.

The codependent movement identified the problems of people who give away their power, people who give too much. Participants in this movement began to draw wise conclusions: They said that people who relate to troubled partners shouldn't tolerate abuse. They should stop subordinating their own needs. They should stop trying to fix their partners. If their partners wanted to change, they would need to make that decision themselves. Therefore, they concluded, codependent people should shift their focus toward doing what they could about improving their own behavior. They needed to consider their own needs, express their feelings, and learn self-assertion, which for them was no small challenge.

Because drug-dependent people are needy and demanding, it's not surprising that the subservient role and the resulting power imbalance were first widely recognized in these families. Eventually it expanded to include people involved with any partners who had almost any serious behavior problem.

Even as codependent people began to understand their own participation in relationship problems, there has always been an element of victimization in the analysis, a sense of "poor me." It is as if the real blame belonged to the abuses of the partners. Sure, the codependent person had to change, but the solutions centered on changing in response to the problem person, not the couple changing together. This left out one important possibility: that partners could see their mutual problems and work as a team to correct them. It also tended to blame the "other person" and minimize the responsibility of the codependent one. In other words, the codependent movement has led to too much complaining and too little cooperation.

From a broader perspective, it is clear that the "codependent" pattern of putting aside one's own needs and focusing on a partner is *not* limited to relationships with individuals having serious behavioral problems. In our competitive society, many people have been trained to accept a one-down position. Codependence, or more to the point, subservient behavior, takes place in a wide cross section of relationships. This phenomenon can be best understood as part of a much larger problem: the inability of people to share power and cooperate as equals.

Those who have been involved in the codependent movement can gain greater clarity in their thinking by looking at the larger picture of competition. People who call themselves codependent, and many others who may not use the terminology but want to stop enduring the pain of subordination, can strive toward the cooperative vision of a relationship that you will see in the love stories in this book. You will see that people are trained either to compete for power or to surrender power. The challenge for a successful relationship is to learn to share power as equals.

BREAKING OUT OF THE COMPETITIVE MODE

As I mentioned, when I tell lecture and workshop audiences about Arthur's "reasonable" power play, their recommendations for Sharon are almost always extremely harsh. Most audience members recommend that she dump the guy. The more tolerant ones suggest that she should "let him have it," or as others put it, "lower the boom." The indignation about Arthur's self-centered behavior is understandable, but the recommendations reflect how difficult people find it to imagine reasonable and respectful communication that could resolve competitive struggles, work out differences, and *equalize* power. Just as Sharon and Arthur were in a competitive struggle, so audiences see things in a competitive way. They want to help Sharon—the oppressed victim—win the battle. They don't think about cooperation and breaking the cycle of competition. Instead of encouraging Sharon assertively to engage in a dialogue and working toward a harmonious relationship, they say she should end it all. But if she dumps him, she would never learn to assert herself as an equal. She would be unprepared for future relationships. She also would never find out if Arthur and she could have changed for the better.

I'm not suggesting that Sharon shouldn't be angry. She should, and she must tell Arthur. She also must assert her needs. Until she asserts herself as an equal, she is a willing partner in the problem. However, assertively expressing herself is not the same as "letting him have it" or "dumping him." Tossing him away does not equalize the power distribution. It ends the relationship.

What could Sharon have done differently with Arthur? When he got pushy on the phone, she could have attempted to nip the problem in the bud with a statement such as this:

"Wait a minute. You're interrupting me and jumping to conclusions. Let me finish what I'm saying and explain my thoughts."

Then she could have reasserted her needs and said that she wanted to work out an agreement that they *both* would find acceptable.

If she didn't immediately recognize his power play while she was on the phone, she could have called him back afterward or spoken to him in person to explain what happened. For example:

"When I called you this morning it was because I had an important job opportunity that I wanted to discuss with you. Before I finished talking, you interrupted me. You implied that I was selfish. Then you listed five reasons why I should do what you wanted me to do. You didn't bother to listen to me. I had some good ideas about what we could do. I think we each had important needs this morning. I wish you had paid attention to mine. Before I could make any suggestions about a ride to the airport, you shifted the focus to what you needed. You ignored me. I think we *both* could have been happy. I think we could have found a creative solution to our problem. But you didn't listen. You pushed for what you wanted. And I made the mistake of giving in. I shouldn't have done that."

Then she might have insisted on making new arrangements for the ride the next day, or could have sought an agreement that they would do things differently in the future.

Was it likely that Sharon could have done this easily? No. Was it likely that Arthur would have quickly understood? No. He probably would have been quite defensive. But if they were going to have a high-quality, loving, cooperative relationship, they needed to change their attitudes and learn some new skills. If Sharon had been assertive about her needs, it would have been a step in the right direction. Instead of accepting a negative status quo, it would have represented a correct move. Someone has to start the process of change.

In some of the other love stories you'll see examples of how people in subservient positions asserted themselves to solve problems and equalize power in their relationships. You'll see more of the type of dialogue that Sharon could have used with Arthur, and how she could have persisted if she had so chosen.

PAYING ATTENTION TO YOUR PARTNER

Several months after the airport ride incident, Sharon came for counseling to discuss her decision—that was final—to end the relationship with Arthur. For her, it had been a gradual realization that her personal needs had been subordinated. It so happened that the ride to the airport was the particular incident that began to awaken her to a problem.

Apparently Arthur told Sharon that her decision to break up was a big surprise. "You never gave me any warnings," he complained as he endured what happens to so many people who have been involved with an unassertive partner who feels increasingly dissatisfied.

Arthur was right that there had been no overt warning signs that something was wrong. But there were certain indicators that he shouldn't have overlooked. The potential for a big surprise is always great: (1) if a partner doesn't ask for what he or she wants and (2) doesn't express criticism, resentment, or other negative feelings. Sharon was unassertive in both these ways.

But it takes two to make the big surprise. One person is unassertive. The other—in this case, Arthur—merrily rolls along, getting most of what he wants and failing to notice that his partner is lost in the shuffle.

If you have an unassertive partner, you can avoid the big surprise by taking preventive measures such as *insisting* that your partner state his or her preferences before family decisions are made. Although an occasional "I don't care" or "Whatever you want" can be accepted, a steady diet of this response spells trouble in the long run.

Also you should be sure that your partner feels free to express criticism and negative feelings. If these thoughts and feelings are withheld, you need to actively encourage that they be communicated.

There's a more positive, less defensive way to think about preventing the big surprise. If you consistently pay lots of loving attention to your partner, check how he or she is doing on a regular basis, and know for a fact that he or she is happy, then you'll never experience the shock of the big surprise. One way to do this is regularly to ask your partner questions such as these: What do you feel? What do you want? Is anything bothering you? How can I make you happier? How can we make the relationship better?

These questions help unassertive people get their needs and feelings into the open. Asking them questions is a way to keep power and benefits equal in a relationship, even if your partner is inclined toward a subordinate position.

GUIDELINES FOR COOPERATION

When a dominant person and a submissive person meet, at first it looks like a perfect match. Decisions are made without conflict. Disagreements are few. The two roles complement each other. People accept and even embrace the inequality without realizing it. Historically it has been men in the dominant position, although women also can play this role. Women tend to be less comfortable with the dominant position, and sometimes are told that they are "playing the male role."

This sort of unfair relationship—as you have seen—feels cozy at first but is unstable in the long run. Equality and cooperation are the *fair* ways to make a loving relationship and also happen to provide the most stability.

Three simple yet challenging guidelines for cooperative relationships can help you avoid unconsciously slipping into the easily accepted roles of dominance or submission:
1. Say what you think and feel. This means keeping no secrets. It includes asking for 100 percent of what you want; saying what bothers you; and saying what feels good.
2. No rescues; don't give away your power. No power plays; don't grab power and try to dominate.
3. Listen to each other; then negotiate with equality and fairness in mind.

Guideline number one surprises many people. At first, the idea of asking for everything you want sounds selfish. But notice that the rule says to ask, not to demand, and not to grab. If a couple wants to meet each other halfway, then they need to know the starting points. That is why both people should ask for what they want.

People who do not ask make a relationship one-sided. By "self-bargaining" they make concessions before negotiations begin and deprive themselves of full representation during the negotiating process. They also deny their partners the pleasure of fully satisfying their needs. Remember: People in cooperative relationships *want* to satisfy each other.

Once both individuals say what they want, a couple must stay alert to behavior that would send the relationship on a competitive course. Consequently the second guideline for cooperation is: no rescues and no power plays. In other words, neither person gives away all the power. That would be a rescue. Neither one attempts to seize the power or to coerce the other. That would be a power play.

People rescue by simply conceding or giving in all the time. In so doing, they "save" the other person from disappointment. Rescuing behavior is frequently misperceived as cooperative. But giving in is not a cooperative option if an attempt wasn't first made to find a solution that would fully satisfy everyone. It's also not a cooperative option if the same person almost always makes the concessions. Such an imbalance indicates a lack of mutual respect.

Giving in represents a loving and cooperative way to resolve a disagreement *only* if there is no good solution that could satisfy everyone, and if each person is willing to make concessions of this sort from time to time.

Power plays are used for control and domination in a relationship. They undermine cooperation. They can be anything from the use of force or the threat of the use of force, to the use of emotional threats, such as the manipulation of guilt or the quiet impact of "the big sulk." Arthur simply used his ability to outtalk Sharon in his demand for a ride to the airport.

Power plays are often motivated by fear and mistrust: People are afraid that they'll be cheated if they don't push hard for themselves. Sometimes power plays are deliberate and conscious attempts to dominate; at other times they're an automatic, unconscious response to conflict.

Because so much of our cultural training is to use power plays to resolve conflict, we often do it without conscious awareness. Arthur never thought he was trying to dominate Sharon when he argued for a ride to the airport. He thought he was just sticking up for his rights. He thought he was being self-protective. People such as Arthur often confuse assertiveness, which means sticking up for themselves, with aggressiveness, which means forcefully fighting for what they want.

In our culture we are "wired" for competition. Agreeing to the guideline of "no rescues and no power plays" doesn't mean that couples will immediately master the art of cooperation. Rather, it means that they understand that rescues and power plays are impediments to cooperation. They agree to be alert to these competitive behaviors and to work toward reducing their prevalence. They commit themselves to constructively scrutinizing their own and their partner's behavior. They point out when they think a partner is rescuing or using a power play. And they take responsibility for their own behavior when they find themselves rescuing or abusing power.

Once people disavow the competitive mode to resolve conflict, they have only one method left: respectful negotiation. The third guideline for cooperation calls for fair-minded problem-solving. The goal is for members of a couple to satisfy each other. The options are compromise, trade-offs, and creative solutions. With a cooperative vision and a basic cooperative agreement, couples can master the skill of cooperative negotiation. You'll see this in other love stories.

But first we have to face the fact that we've been trained to feel comfortable in a one-up or one-down position with each other. It is hard to be equal, to coordinate needs. That's why I say it takes super skills to transcend our competitive training and to establish cooperative, loving relationships. You'll learn about the super skills in the next love story.

CHAPTER
5

Super Skills

David became an instant father when he married Susan three years ago and adopted her two daughters, seven and twelve years old. It was a big change for everyone in the new family, but they adjusted well. David enthusiastically embraced his parental responsibilities. The kids slowly but gradually warmed up to their stepdad. Susan was pleased that her new husband was very much a family man, because commitment to family was one of her important values.

David's parents are what is locally referred to as "snowbirds"—that is, people who migrate in flocks to the warm and sunny Arizona climate when the winter temperatures drop and the snow begins to fall in the East and Midwest. His parents had been making month-long winter migrations for many years, in part to see David, who lives in Tucson. During their stay they would spend almost every evening with their son, and now that he was married, with him and his family.

One week into the most recent visit, Susan began to feel uneasy. She wanted more privacy and time alone with her husband and children. She thought about the previous two visits and remembered also having felt crowded, but not saying anything about it. She recalled that David was unhappy and complained of feeling "too responsible" for his parents. Each time, David and she had felt tense and overwhelmed almost the entire visit.

"Can we ask your parents to give us a couple of nights alone each week?" she asked David. "They're great people, really, but it's been too intense for me. I think we need some time for us and the kids. What do you think?"

Knowing how Susan felt about family, it came as a surprise to David, and angered him, that she had objections to the time with his parents. He thought that Susan was selfish, ignoring that the visit was important to him. Anyway, it wasn't as if his parents had imposed themselves on the family. David invited them and had encouraged a long visit—all with Susan's blessing.

"Why are you so damn selfish?" David said in an unquestionably harsh tone. "These are my parents you're talking about. They've always visited in the winter. I've always looked forward to it. Now that we're married, it seems like you want to tell me what I can and can't do. This is ridiculous."

As he continued to speak, more intensity came into his voice. He was practically yelling at one point, with a harshness that seemed out of character.

"Sometimes I think," David concluded, "that you're very selfish and controlling."

"Don't call me selfish," Susan answered. "I simply told you what I feel about your parents' visit. Don't go calling me names. You know (pause), I'm seeing a mean streak in you that I never knew about. Would you please try to calm yourself down?"

"Yeah, right," David answered, "me calm down. I'm just making an observation. It seems that when *your children* or *your parents* are involved, you ask me to accommodate them.

You think family is important. But with *my parents*, it's a different story."

David felt that he had been wronged. Susan said what she wanted, and now he felt he had to comply. It was a control issue.

"I don't even want to be around you. You really make me sick. You know, at times like these, I think I should have stayed with Karen [a longtime girlfriend from the past]. At least she seemed to care about my feelings. You don't. You're all caught up in yourself and your own feelings. Then you have the nerve to tell *me* to calm down. Of course I'm upset. Look at what you're saying about my parents. You're acting like a real bitch."

Even as he said this last statement, he thought he shouldn't. But then he thought about how very "wronged" he felt.

"Don't go calling me a bitch," Susan answered.

"I'm not calling you a bitch," David replied, "I'm just saying that you're acting like one right now."

Their argument took a variety of twists and turns before they eventually appeared in my office a week later, both of them alarmed that their relationship could unravel so quickly. Meanwhile, they hid their argument from David's parents as best they could. It was a tense situation.

Both David and Susan knew they shouldn't behave in ways they would later regret. Neither of them liked what was happening. Both were uncomfortable with the hostile tone that now characterized their interactions. Both intuitively understood the importance of the super decision—which means committing yourself to being careful to avoid unnecessarily hurting the people you love. That's why, sensing that something was wrong, they had quickly come for help. Even though David felt justified about his rage as it had erupted, and for the most part afterward, he still felt uneasy about it. He knew that his tone had been threatening. On the other hand, he was outraged by Susan. He felt she deserved his anger.

I told Susan and David of the importance of formally agreeing to cooperate as a team in the spirit of "one for all and all for one." On an intellectual level they understood the importance of making a Basic Cooperative Agreement (BCA). But on an emotional level, David had problems with the agreement. He doubted Susan's willingness to cooperate. He saw her as selfish. How could she now agree to cooperate, he asked, when she had been so selfish about his parents' visit? It seemed hypocritical.

Susan answered by saying that she was disillusioned about David. He had seemed so mild-mannered and nonthreatening, yet become so vicious. His anger scared her.

I explained to David that if Susan said she wanted to cooperate, he needed to trust her. The agreement to cooperate doesn't preclude either of them making mistakes, and sometimes even behaving selfishly. If Susan had been uncooperative, I assured him, she would recognize this in the course of a reasonable discussion, and then apologize. By the same token, an agreement to cooperate also means that one must fully consider the other person's point of view, whether you agree with it or not. *Self-certainty—being totally sure that you are right and your partner is wrong—does not make for cooperativeness.* I warned David that people often become overcommitted to their own "rightness." It is fine to be self-assured—that is, confident about oneself—but a terrible error to be self-certain.

Neither David nor Susan wanted to fight. They wanted cooperation, but clearly each of them lacked the skills to realize their vision. Because we are so geared toward competitiveness in this society, good intentions are not enough to sustain a cooperative, loving relationship. From childhood, we are encouraged and conditioned to compete. Competitiveness is highly valued. It is the norm. It is the automatic, normal reaction to conflict. Competitive behavior is also reinforced in the day-to-day work world. Even people who want warm, cooperative relationships find it hard to transform themselves into soft, sensitive human beings after spending eight hours in a competitive work environment. Yet we need to be warm, sensitive, and cooperative with the people we love.

For couples to succeed in cooperative relationships, they have to transcend both lifelong conditioning to compete and the daily reinforcement of competitive behavior. They have to learn the skills of cooperation. Mastery of these skills requires enormous effort, discipline, and determination. That's why I call them the *super skills*. David and Susan started with cooperative intentions, but needed to master the super skills to solve their relationship problems and to maintain their basic goodwill.

THE SUPER CHALLENGE

Listening to David and Susan blame each other for their dispute, I decided to start by introducing them to the *super challenge*. I explained: *When two people argue, usually each person thinks that he or she is right and the other is wrong.* That's the nature of arguments. One exception to this is extremely self-centered people, who argue for the sake of winning, even when they know they're wrong. Another exception is well-intentioned people who, at their worst moments, argue without good cause. But this is not the norm, and was not the case with Susan and David.

David argued because he thought that Susan was being selfish by complaining about his parents' visit.

Susan thought that David was not acting like a responsible adult toward her and the children by spending every evening with his parents. She was also very upset about David's aggressive behavior toward her.

I explained the super challenge to them. It has two parts:
1. *Learn to question yourself. Realize that your opinion (or position) is not necessarily right, no matter how certain you are of yourself. Accept the possibility that you could*

even be wrong. Bear in mind that the other person may be equally certain of his position.
2. *Don't assume that the other person (your partner) is wrong. Look for the validity in what your partner is saying.* Your partner probably wouldn't be arguing unless he thought he was right.

When I present this concept to people, I suggest that they take a statistical perspective in their thinking. If only one person is right in an argument, each person should assume, unless he is arrogant, that he would be right about half the time and wrong the other half.

I also explained to David and Susan that in many arguments the truth lies halfway between what the two people think. Neither person is exactly wrong and neither is exactly right.

Then I said that, with surprising frequency, couples argue about something that is not at all a matter of one person being right and the other one wrong. Often both points of view have merit. Both could be right. When this occurs, the couple must find a way to respect two different but valid viewpoints. Unfortunately, people usually don't recognize these situations and misdefine them as competitive, with each person trying to outargue and prove the other one wrong.

I gave David and Susan a graphic fictional example, complete with quotes, of a marital conflict in which both people were "right." I thought it was a good example for them because the argument involved in-laws, which was also part of their disagreement. At issue was where this fictional couple would spend a Thanksgiving holiday, and also how to allocate family funds. This is how I described the argument:

The husband said, "It's stupid to think we could have a good time with your mother visiting during Thanksgiving. She would be telling me that I'm a failure and telling you that the turkey and vegetables are overcooked."

The wife answered, "So you want to go back to Boston and be with your parents and visit that zoo. I especially like it when your grandmother starts throwing food.

"It's also a question of money," she continued. "You don't seem to care that our house is a mess. At least if we stayed home we could afford to have someone paint the walls and install new carpets."

The husband replied, "There you go again spending our money competing with the neighbors for 'nice house' awards. You never want to do anything that might be fun."

In this argument, each person was trying to prevail by discrediting the other one's point of view, first about family, then about finances and recreation.

If instead of competing they had taken the super challenge, they would have recognized the validity of each other's point of view. The husband would have realized that his wife was not wrong. She wanted her mother to visit, regardless of her shortcomings. Also, she wanted to invest their limited financial resources on household repairs. Those were her priorities. If the wife had taken the super challenge, she would have realized that her husband was not wrong. He wanted to visit his parents in Boston, no matter what his grandmother might do and what the trip would cost. These were his priorities. Both husband and wife are entitled to individual preferences and personal values about family and finances.

Rather than bickering and trying to discredit each other, this couple's energy would be better spent in respectfully negotiating as a team to find a fair solution to their differences, one they both could accept. The ideal solution would be a compromise, or a trade-off: Your way this time. My way next time.

Conflict such as this can be temporarily settled, but never adequately resolved, by one person bullying or outarguing the other. To add flair to my fictional account, I tacked on a dramatic ending:

"Well," the husband said a few days after the Thanksgiving argument, "I bought the airplane tickets for our visit to Boston and they're nonrefundable." (It looks as though he won the battle.)

"Fine," his wife answered. "Better bring along some people who like you. I'm staying home with the kids."

After telling this story, I explained to David and Susan that when couples are in conflict, one person can't totally ignore the other's argument. Each person has to try to recognize the validity of the other's perspective.

At this point, David protested. He said he was willing to accept that he was wrong half the time in his arguments with Susan. But this particular incident was clear-cut, black-and-white. He said Susan was being undeniably selfish: She claimed to be a family person but wanted to limit the visit of his parents. "That's just not fair," he said. "I admit I'm wrong sometimes. But not this time."

What David didn't realize was that Susan could make the same claim in reverse, that she was right and that he was wrong. She could say that all she ever did was *suggest* that his parents not visit every night. She didn't say that they couldn't. It was a suggestion. And it wasn't selfish. It was as much for David and the children as it was for herself. Therefore David had started a fight, complete with name-calling, over absolutely nothing.

But, I stressed to the two of them, the idea of the super challenge is to get away from this type of simplistic thinking. In an argument it is too easy and too lazy to assume that you are right and the other person is wrong. And you can get really worked up about it, too.

The super challenge makes people go counter to their gut feelings. If you are sure you are right, you will not tend to be interested in what the other person thinks. But that causes serious problems. So you must calm yourself down and listen to your partner.

The worst danger of not taking the super challenge is that sometimes people feel so self-certain that they can justify anything. Feeling this way, they hurt the people they say they love, and justify it by saying, "I was right. You were wrong. You forced me to do this." The mind plays funny tricks. It gets us doing things we shouldn't do, and feeling all right about it.

SUPER CALMNESS

People are usually upset and emotionally aroused at precisely the moments they need to take the super challenge. So you might wonder how they could ever succeed in mastering this skill. The answer is that they must be capable of *super calmness: This means having the self-control not to misbehave toward a partner when you are under stress.*

Imagine that you're driving a car in New York City, late for an appointment, and lost. You're trying to make a right-hand turn, but throngs of pedestrians block your path. Your spouse is navigating with a map, but confused, saying, "I'm not sure which way we should go." In the rearview mirror you see an enormous Mack truck, almost larger than life, right up against the trunk of your car. The truck driver blasts his horn.

Under stress such as this and during times of crisis, many people have the tendency to get impatient, to bark at their partners, and to start fights. They take out their frustrations on each other. They blame each other. They feel isolated and alone. They don't know how to provide mutual support. Yet these are precisely the times when couples need to stay calm and work as a team.

Super calmness means to "stay cool." You make a choice to remain a supportive team instead of taking out your frustrations on each other by getting grouchy, short-tempered, or hypercritical. When you're in a New York City traffic jam, you remember that you're in it together. You might even smile or make a joke. A sense of humor is priceless. In other words, when you're under stress, don't compound the problem by taking it out on each other.

Super calmness should be practiced in any stressful situation. It applies when you're up all night caring for a baby; when there's a financial crunch; and when you both come home from work at five o'clock and someone has to prepare a meal. And certainly it applies when the in-laws are in town visiting, as was the case with David's snowbird parents.

I pointed out to David and Susan that both of them said they felt stress when his parents visited. They needed to stay calm and work as a team. I told them that super calmness means *not* taking out frustrations on your partner. You have to remind yourself of the super decision: your commitment to be fair and to behave well. You also have to keep in mind the love you feel for your partner, and the senselessness of doing something that is hurtful.

SUPER DISCIPLINE

When people feel that they have been "wronged" by someone they love, they find it especially difficult to stay calm. To maintain super calmness in these situations, you need another skill: *super discipline. When you feel wronged, super discipline means to explain calmly with care what you think and feel, remembering that the purpose of communication in a cooperative relationship is to love and support each other.*

With super discipline you refrain from panicked retaliation or from using what you perceive to be a partner's poor behavior to be an excuse to behave poorly yourself. Even if you feel the urge to respond in a forceful way, you resist temptation. Conflict doesn't have to mean pitching a tent for battle.

In the heat of an argument, people sometimes take actions they later regret. The most extreme is physical violence. The next extreme is saying something horrible they eventually wish they had never said. Less dramatic, but still harmful, are hurtful and aggressive comments that slip out. Apologies may follow, but the damage is done.

The regretted action usually seems right at the moment. The people who unleash the aggression believe they have been misunderstood or mistreated or wronged. They think the best way to correct the injustice is to strike with great force. They feel alone, without connection to the people they love. They forget that they are part of a couple or family. They forget that they care about the feelings of the other person. They think, "I've got to stick up for myself. I've got to right this wrong."

At these moments, intense and often exaggerated hurt thoughts and feelings frantically rush through their minds:
- Why did you do this to me?
- How could you be so thoughtless?
- You've done this so many times before (this may or may not be true).
- You're selfish.
- This is unforgivable.
- I'd never do this to you.

This is exactly what happened with David first, and then Susan. David felt wronged because his wife, who claimed to be a family person, had "selfishly and thoughtlessly" asked him to spend less time with his parents. He felt this was awful and that he needed to act quickly and forcefully to correct it.

I call it *false power* whenever people in loving relationships get the idea that a power play can quickly right an injustice. People huff and puff with false power and make their problems worse. David only made matters worse when he accused Susan of selfishness.

Then Susan felt wronged by David's tone of voice and aggressive words. Her response was more disciplined than his, but still accusatory when she talked about his "mean streak."

I explained to this couple that super discipline is the opposite of playground logic, or playground justice. In the playground, if one child throws mud, the other throws mud back. When the two children come home covered with mud—each blaming the other—it's impossible to get to the bottom of the problem. Regardless of who started it (which may not be evident), each had thrown mud.

I told David and Susan that even if one of them was wrong, they still needed to stay calm and talk with each other respectfully and calmly. That's how they could fix the problem. And I reminded them of the super challenge, not to be so certain that they were right.

Super discipline is crucial to maintaining goodwill and harmony in a relationship. Let's face it: From time to time the people we love make mistakes. Even the most loving people are sometimes out of sorts. If we respond in kind to a partner's worst behavior, then we have two people doing the wrong things, and no one trying to restore positive behavior. The same could be said in reverse. When we make mistakes or misbehave, if our partners retaliate, we will have a serious problem. Super discipline means to rise above pettiness and hold firm to the cooperative path. It means you don't panic when faced with normal human fallibility. You are tolerant.

Most of the really bad things that people do to each other are done in a moment of passion with some sort of justification. An abusive husband doesn't say, "I hit my wife. I'm a bad guy." Instead he claims, "She provoked me." Even murderers usually have a rationale for their actions.

SUPER OPEN MIND

If you've taken the super challenge and you're not assuming that you are necessarily right, nor that your partner is necessarily wrong, then you need to do some serious *work in understanding what may be wrong about your own point of view and right about your partner's*. This means keeping a *super open mind*. It means you seek and are receptive to points of view other than those you now hold.

I told David and Susan that they needed to sharpen their listening and communication skills, and I introduced them to a couple of important techniques.

One of them I call *the pause*. It simply means to wait a few seconds before responding to something your partner says. After the other person speaks, you take time to think about what was said before you say anything. The pause counteracts a natural tendency to become defensive and to reject an "opposing" point of view quickly.

Another way to sharpen listening skills is by *paraphrasing*. This means to say back what was said in different words to make sure you understand the communication. When you paraphrase, you don't challenge or disagree. You simply try to grasp the meaning of what was said, as in: "Let me see if I understand what you are saying. It sounds as if . . ."

Next I suggested to David and Susan that they try an exercise that requires super discipline. The exercise is called "Speaking and Hard Listening." In this exercise each person takes up to five minutes to explain his point of view, and the other paraphrases what was said for clarification and to avoid any misunderstandings. There are no interruptions. While one person speaks, the other tries to hear the validity of what is being said. He tries to put himself in the speaker's shoes, to see a different reality.

When David spoke, he explained that he was very hurt by Susan's idea of spending less time with his parents. He thought it was selfish and thoughtless. He also said it would be very difficult for him to tell his parents not to spend every evening with them. Never before had he requested distance from them.

Susan interrupted when David said she was "selfish." I reminded her that it is important to find the validity in what was said, and neither to take offense nor to look for distortions. She calmed herself down and continued to listen. She did a good job of paraphrasing what David said. She also added that she had not realized how hard it would be for him to tell his parents not to spend all their time with David and her.

When it was Susan's turn to speak, she told David that her motivation for time away from his parents was for everyone's welfare, including his. She reminded him of how upset and exhausted he had been during previous visits. She also said she wanted time apart for their children's sake, and admitted that she wanted the space for herself as well. She reaffirmed her love and appreciation of David's parents. She also told David that she was hurt and scared when he started raising his voice and calling her selfish.

David did a surprisingly good job of paraphrasing what Susan had said. Apparently he had been helped by all the talk about cooperation, the super decision, the super skills, and reminding yourself that your partner loves you.

Once the two of them listened to each other, working out their immediate problem was relatively easy. David realized that Susan was making a good point about not spending all their time together with his parents. He saw it was in everybody's best interest. He even thought that his parents might want some time to themselves.

Susan realized how hard it was for David to speak to his parents on this topic, especially in light of past history.

In the end, David and Susan decided to deal with the problem in a subtle way this visit, by asking his parents to baby-sit a couple of times to help them "get out," and by buying his parents tickets to some of the cultural events they would enjoy. David and Susan decided that before the next visit they would talk with his parents in a loving way about making different arrangements. It would be difficult for David, but he thought it was the right thing to do.

The biggest lesson from this fight was that they needed to learn super discipline. We talked extensively about *not* assuming the worst about your partner and about giving the benefit of the doubt. Then we spent a couple of weeks talking about better communication techniques for cooperative relationships. We also worked on inner insecurities that led the two of them to panic. In particular David realized that he was frightened that his parents would disapprove of Susan as "pushy" if he were to ask for time away from them. He was overly concerned about their approval. Susan found that she hit the roof whenever anyone called her "selfish," because that label had been unfairly used against her as a child.

As Susan and David learned the super skills, their relationship continued to grow stronger. Now they are quite happy together. In some of the following love stories there will be more on cooperative communication and on recognizing and overcoming personal insecurities.

CHAPTER 6

Stuck Point

A physician friend called about a patient he was referring, a man in his early fifties. This man's first wife had died tragically eight years earlier in an automobile accident. After sending his children to college and a few years of dating, he had recently remarried. Now his new wife, Margaret, was making him miserable. She was terribly aggressive. She called him "stupid," "dopey," and other names. She threatened to have an affair. She even hit him several times, and for what seemed to be trivial reasons: Once he forgot to bring home the Sunday newspaper. Once he put chocolate cake in the shopping cart at the supermarket, while she was on a diet.

Although my physician friend who made the referral had never met Margaret, he called her a "monster."

John, the prospective client, made an appointment for marriage counseling. The morning of the appointment, Margaret called to cancel. Fifteen minutes later, John called back to say he had just discovered what she had done and that he would like to come alone.

At the appointment, my new client described his wife as a "monster" (the same label used by the referring physician) and presented a case to prove his point. He spoke like a lawyer who had prepared a legal brief in a criminal trial. He put his story in context by explaining that he got along well with his first wife. Therefore it was certain that his current relationship problems must be caused by his current wife, who, he explained, had a temper problem. He then recited the same examples of Margaret's misbehavior that he had told my physician friend, starting with one of the hitting incidents.

After listing his wife's transgressions, he paused, as if waiting for my agreement that his wife indeed was a monster. Then he proceeded.

"What should I do about her?" he asked. "She has ruined our relationship. Can you tell me what to do?"

Although only he came for the appointment, he clearly felt "wronged" and that his wife was the person with the problems.

People like John—who are convinced they have been wronged by a partner—tell their version of their story to friends or professionals expecting to gain confirmation of their positions. It doesn't matter if they come alone or as a couple. Typically they blame their partners for everything and present a well-documented case about his (or her) faults.

Professionals and well-meaning friends sometimes feel pressured to agree: They see people in pain. They want to help. They want to provide comfort. However, the people in pain want them to accept and support their one-sided version of the story uncritically. They want the "helpers" to blame their partners for everything.

My friend, the referring physician, fell into the trap. He had accepted John's point of view that his wife was a "monster," and advised him to end the relationship because "life is short."

The mistake he was making was to accept John's very emotional, possibly angry, possibly hurt view of the relationship. Most people—like John in this case—can clearly label the faults of their partners. But they have not looked at their own part of the problem, nor have they considered their partners' point of view. They certainly have not thought about what *they* could do differently to improve matters. These people want their helpers to agree with them. But when helping people reinforce a distorted, one-sided perspective, they actually *reduce* the likelihood of a couple resolving their problems. They harden people in their positions, making it more difficult for them to gain objectivity—which is exactly what the couple needs to do. People with relationship problems must learn to listen to what their partners want. They have to be self-critical. Conflict can never be settled cooperatively to everyone's satisfaction without considering everyone's point of view.

John was not at all self-critical. He did not mention any of his own mistakes or wrongdoing. He also lacked insight into how his wife might see things. Rather than seeking new insight, he wanted me to support his position.

"You can see," he said, "she's awful. She actually hits me. It makes me so mad. She's a monster."

I was unwilling to jump on the blame bandwagon about his "monster" wife, but did want to validate his feelings because he clearly was upset about his disappointing marriage.

"I'm sorry," I said, "that you hurt so much. I know it must be awful to be hit by your wife. It's good you didn't hit back, because violence is no solution."

"I felt like hitting back," John said, "but I'm not that sort of guy."

"Good for you," I answered. "And it's good you came here to work on things. It's important to solve these problems."

With these comments I was able to give John emotional support without compromising my objectivity and accepting a "good guy" (him) versus "bad guy" (his wife) point of view. I didn't want to harden his position. But John still wanted more. He wanted me to agree that his wife was a monster and the cause of all their problems. He kept pushing the point.

"You can see how awful she is, can't you? She's so aggressive. I'm just a quiet, easygoing guy. She's really hard to take. I don't know what to do about her."

I said I could see why he was so upset by some of the things she had done, but added that Margaret must have some *good* qualities. Something must have attracted him. Otherwise he wouldn't have married her. This was my first attempt at challenging his hardened position about Margaret being totally bad. John paused, somewhat taken aback by my comments. He seemed to soften momentarily, and talked of some of the fun they had enjoyed together. He also said Margaret could be very sweet when she wasn't angry. Then he started with some "buts" and gradually worked himself back into his disgruntled state, and finally back to building his case.

"I'm sure," I said, "she must have her side to this story." I was beginning to prepare him for the very real task of gaining objectivity.

THE OTHER SIDE OF THE STORY

When people talk about their relationship problems, it's important to ask questions, including tough ones, to help them get in touch with their partners' point of view. Eventually the goal is for them to learn to ask themselves these questions.

"Why," I asked John, "was Margaret so angry about you putting chocolate cake in the shopping cart?"

"I don't know."

"Did you ask her why she hit you?"

"Yes."

"What did she say?"

"She said, 'Because of your German ways.' "

"You see," he continued, "I come from a German family."

"What did she mean by it?"

"I don't know."

"Did you ask her?"

"No. She always says that thing about my German ways. Whatever it means, it doesn't justify hitting me."

I had to agree that hitting was inappropriate, but suggested that he needed to find out what his wife meant by his "German ways."

She should stop hitting, but that wouldn't solve the problem. John still had to find out what was bothering Margaret.

As we continued to talk, I heard about another of Margaret's hot-tempered incidents. She had hit John when he didn't bring home the Sunday newspaper after his brunch with friends. He had apologized for the oversight about the paper, but asked her, and now me, why she had become so violent. He told me how horrified he was by the violence: "No one has ever hit me before." Again her only explanation was that her anger was caused by his "German ways."

STUCK POINT

In their disputes, John and Margaret had stumbled on their *stuck point*. This is the moment at which discussions that should continue instead stop. The discussion ends prematurely, without resolution. Because the conflict is never resolved, the same types of fights recur, ending each time at the same or similar stuck points.

As John and I talked, I began to see that Margaret and he usually reached their stuck point right after Margaret would take some sort of aggressive action, such as hitting him (or threatening to file for divorce, or threatening to have an affair, or calling him names). John would demand an explanation. She would accuse him of behaving in his "German ways." At this point he would quietly leave the room, feeling very angry. She would drop the subject and allow him to leave. The discussion ended. They were stuck.

For them finally to settle their differences, they would have to get past their stuck point and continue the discussion. They had to talk until they understood each other and resolved their differences.

Most couples, like John and Margaret, get stuck in their discussion without realizing what is happening. They stop talking with nothing settled. To reverse the trend, first they need to *know* that they are stuck. Then they need to understand how they got stuck and, finally, how to get past their stuck point.

You can determine how couples get stuck by analyzing their arguments. Certain basic patterns are as follows:

• *One person (or both) withdraws physically from the scene.* It can be an angry or hurt withdrawal. It can be quiet or loud. It can be with or without tears, with or without threats, with or without raised voices. The person who withdraws can leave peacefully or can storm out in a huff, perhaps making a threat about divorce, an affair, suicide, or something else.

• *One person (or both) withdraws emotionally.* They may stay in the physical presence of each other but leave emotionally. "I won't talk about this anymore. We never get anywhere. The discussion just goes on and on. I'm gonna stay here and read my newspaper." A different type of emotional withdrawal is to sulk, which is a passive power play designed to make the other person capitulate. The extreme example of emotional withdrawal is when one person falls asleep during a conversation.

• *Someone changes the subject.* A couple may move on to a more peaceful topic or to an entirely different argument, thus changing the subject. Some couples end an argument by saying, "At least we love each other." These words sound good but resolve nothing.

• *Someone says, "I don't care."* One person indicates (by words or deeds) that he is not interested in the concerns of the other person. He may even throw it back and say, "If you're upset, then it's your problem." The other person accepts this response and lets it slide.

- *One person gives in.* That person starts to think, "Why bother? It's not worth it. He made up his mind. He never listens to me. I'll do it his way."
- *The discussion fizzles.* The conversation gradually dwindles. Less and less is said until silence prevails. They just stop talking.
- *The couple finds a distraction.* One distraction is sex. They may make love and drop the argument. Another distraction is expressing hurt feelings and then being soothed. One person cries and the other gives comfort (or leaves in disgust) without ever dealing with the problem.
- *The couple arrives at a pseudo-resolution.* They appear to settle the conflict, but don't. For example, one person apologizes, not really meaning it. Another pseudoresolution is to say, "We'll finish this discussion later," but then never return to it.
- *A poor solution is accepted to make peace.* This happens when someone makes compromises and concessions in excess of what is personally acceptable in order to end the conflict. It is premature closure. Sooner or later that person will fail to follow through because the agreement was untenable from the start. Then there will be two problems: the initial conflict that was never really settled, plus a broken agreement.

Many couples reach their stuck point so often that they have piles of unfinished discussions. Major issues about how to live together are never resolved.

One twist to the stuck point is that couples can get *stuck before they start*. This happens when they are too frightened even to talk about their problems with each other. They avoid open discussion altogether.

It isn't really surprising that couples reach a stuck point in their arguments. This is a function of our competitive training. Lacking a cooperative vision and cooperative skills—especially the skills of cooperative communication and negotiations—people struggle along as best they can. Because they do not know how to settle conflict, the discussion eventually breaks down.

The stuck point shouldn't be confused with the decision to drop little disputes and let go of minor resentments or hurt feelings. This happens when people recognize that a particular difference of opinion can't be resolved, and are willing to drop it. Both persons acknowledge that they see things differently. They respectfully allow for the differences. No one wins or loses. At this point they can smile at each other and let go of lingering negative feelings. Essentially they resolve the difference by agreeing to drop it. It is a negotiated settlement.

The stuck point also shouldn't be confused with the decision to discontinue a discussion temporarily until a specified time in the future. Many problems cannot be resolved in one "sitting." People need to take a break and resume the discussion later with a fresh start.

ONE-SIDED THINKING

Listening to John at his first counseling session, you would think his marital problems were all Margaret's fault. She hit him and took other aggressive actions—not exactly the sort of behavior you look for in a cooperative relationship. As I listened to John, I still didn't know what his role was in all this turmoil, although I did know he took a totally one-sided, black-and-white view of the dispute. That was certainly part of the problem.

I explained the idea of a stuck point to John. I told him that couples can't leave conflict unresolved indefinitely without eventually drifting apart. They can't allow themselves to get stuck. They have to keep talking until they understand their problems and resolve them. I pointed out that he never found out what was bothering Margaret when she talked about his "German ways." Nothing was settled when he would withdraw angrily. He might have thought the matter was settled, but he was stuck and angry; she was stuck and hurt. The problem did not disappear and would not go away until they could settle their differences in a way that was acceptable to both of them.

"Do you understand?" I asked.

"Yes," he said, "but she hits me. That's inexcusable."

He seemed determined to keep Margaret as the "bad guy." I asked him why he had come to therapy. Did he want to work things out, or was he looking for support to break up?

"No, no," he said. "I believe in working things out with a partner. I just don't know if it's possible with a wife like Margaret."

I took his continued one-sidedness as a poor prognosis for the marriage. It didn't look good. But I continued and said, "Let's see if we can figure out what causes these problems."

WHAT WAS BOTHERING MARGARET?

I told John that his wife must have something in mind when she complained about his "German ways." Something was bothering her. He needed to know what it was. I asked about the time she hit him when he didn't bring the newspaper home on Sunday.

"Why do you think Margaret was so angry?"

"I don't know."

"Try hard to think about it. She probably didn't hit you *just* because you forgot the newspaper. Do you often forget to do things you say you will do?"

"No."

"Was anything else bothering Margaret? Had anything else happened that morning?"

"Well, she had complained that I was eating breakfast with my friends. But I already made those plans several days earlier. So there was no way I could change them."

"What was bothering her about your decision?"

"Well, she said she wanted to go out to breakfast with me."

"Had she complained about that before?"

"Yeah, almost every week. She wants to go to breakfast together on Sundays. She says we're never close. We never talk. She drives me nuts with that."

"So it sounds as though she is angry that you don't take her to breakfast on Sundays and that she wants more time and closeness with you. Is that it?"

"Yes. But that doesn't justify hitting me, does it?"

"No, it doesn't. But maybe now we can begin to figure out what she means by your 'German ways.' It sounds as though she sees you as someone who sometimes stubbornly disregards what she wants."

Now we were beginning to uncover the reasons this woman was so angry. From what John was saying, I gathered that Margaret had consistently asked for what she wanted—his companionship on Sunday mornings. He continually ignored her request, and even went out with friends instead. She was probably hurt and angry, and finally lost control over a relatively minor issue—his forgetting to bring the Sunday newspaper.

It was interesting to discover, too, that the other "hitting" incident—when Margaret hit John after he put chocolate cake in the shopping cart—seemed to follow a similar pattern. She was on a diet that he knew about. He had agreed not to bring home high-calorie sweets. Yet one day he brought home ice cream. The next day he brought home candy. It was on the following day that he put chocolate cake in the shopping cart. So she hit him—not a very smart thing to do, but it sounded as though she was angrily fighting back against his stubborn disregard of her needs and of their agreement. It looked that way to me. However, the only way truly to know what Margaret meant by his "German ways" would be to ask her.

As our first session drew to a close, I asked John why Margaret had canceled the appointment at the last minute, and whether she would be willing to come in the future. He said she canceled because of a scheduling problem but that she would come to our next meeting. We set a time.

THE PRICE YOU PAY FOR STAYING STUCK

When couples are stuck in their communication, the same problems keep resurfacing without ever getting resolved. Some couples are willing to continue to go through the motions of having a discussion. Others give up, deciding it's pointless to keep talking. However, they pay a price for their resignation.

In some cases, the problems fester for long periods of time. For example, one couple had major arguments about how to spend their money. Although they finally gave up and stopped talking about their differences, they kept spending money in ways that antagonized each other. Over the years, resentments built, and they drifted further and further apart.

Some couples who stop talking about their differences break up eventually. I counseled a man who had been dating a woman who cried and put herself down every time he told her that something bothered him. This made him feel guilty. He would drop his complaint. Then he would comfort his girlfriend and try to boost her morale. This was their stuck point. Finally he decided that it was useless and too exhausting to ever talk about what bothered him. So he gave up. Pretty soon, however, he ended the relationship because there were so many unresolved problems.

Sometimes the problems that initially caused an unresolved argument pass with time, but the bad feelings remain. I have worked with couples who think back about critical moments in their relationship—ten, twenty, thirty or more years in the past. They see a particular moment as the turning point in a decline of intimacy, or perhaps a pivotal time at which bad feelings began that persisted for many years, as reflected in remarks such as these:

• "Where were you when I lost my job working for IBM? I was so hurt. You didn't even comfort me. That's when I decided you didn't love me. That's when I started to make a totally separate and independent life."

- "Do you remember when you told me you hated my father? It really hurt my feelings. I didn't feel that you cared about me, so I never wanted to give you the things that you wanted from me—from that moment on."

As you can see, couples need to settle their differences. Loose ends and unresolved differences inevitably become barriers to intimacy. When people get stuck, they distance themselves from each other, often with a grudge and lingering resentment.

GETTING PAST A STUCK POINT

Margaret came with John to the second counseling session. I reviewed the concept of the stuck point for John, and introduced it to Margaret. Then I gave a little pep talk, explaining that conflict is inevitable in relationships but that successful couples face their conflict and resolve differences cooperatively. I told them about sunset couples, those people who have been happily married for thirty, forty, fifty or more years. Most of these couples say that they had tough times during the early stages of their marriage. They say they had differences, sometimes serious ones. But they never retreated. The sunset couples had discussions to resolve their conflict. They remained committed to settling their differences. In this context I assured John and Margaret that there is nothing unusual about having serious conflict during the early stages of a relationship. However, I said, they must address and settle their differences.

The key to success is never to let the dialogue end without getting to the bottom of the problem.

This principle applies to couples who tend to let their discussions fizzle out. It applies when one person starts to cry. It applies when a couple starts to change the topic. Someone has to redirect the process in a positive way:

"We can't stop talking. We haven't solved the problem yet."

The couple can take a break from a discussion. They can and should put aside a discussion temporarily if it is not productive. But ultimately they must be persistent and return to the problem until it is solved. If they cannot solve it themselves, they should go for help.

An attitude of persistence does not mean that problems will be solved easily. In fact, most people lack good communication, negotiation, and conflict resolution skills. It is no coincidence that they tend to get stuck. But by stopping the discussion, there is no chance to resolve the matter. The only way to work it out is to face the conflict squarely and to learn to resolve it cooperatively. There is no shortcut.

As we talked, Margaret and John could see how they got stuck: She would lose her temper; he would walk away. One of them needed to stay on target. One of them needed to insist that the dialogue continue.

TWO CHALLENGES

Once couples realize they are stuck, the next challenge is to reopen the discussion. Then comes the biggest challenge, which is to make progress and eventually settle the conflict in a cooperative way.

John and Margaret needed to reopen their discussion. They also needed to learn communication and negotiation skills to solve their problems.

I suggested to them that we backtrack to figure out what was happening.

Without missing a beat, John accused Margaret of causing their problems: "If she wouldn't attack me, I wouldn't walk out on her. No one feels good about talking to someone who threatens to have an affair or sometimes even hits them."

"Oh, I never hurt you when I hit you," Margaret said. "It's more like I'm trying to get your attention. You know that. And you know I'd never have an affair. It's just that I get really angry when you don't listen to me. You don't pay attention to what I'm feeling. If you would listen to me and pay some attention to my feelings, I wouldn't be threatening to have affairs.

"Like the first appointment for counseling," she continued. It seems that John had set up that appointment without consulting her, and accepted a time that didn't fit with her schedule. He didn't check with her first, and didn't tell her about it until the morning of the meeting. At that point, Margaret couldn't change her plans. This peculiar process fully explained the last-minute cancellation. "It's typical," she said. "John made an appointment at a time that I couldn't come. He is self-centered. He simply doesn't pay attention to anyone else's feelings but his own."

John reacted defensively to the accusation of selfishness. He said it's hard to pay attention to the needs of someone who hits him and threatens to have an affair. He kept referring to her wrongdoing and said anyone would be doing what he was doing with a "wife like this."

He continued his defense by talking about his ex-wife. He said he paid attention to her. She never complained. This was interesting because as he told the story of his previous marriage, it sounded as though he was quite controlling and usually got his own way. Apparently his first wife was more compliant than Margaret. In any event, the previous marriage seemed irrelevant. We were not trying to judge John's character. We were not in a court of law. What mattered now was what was happening between John and Margaret, not whether John had been a "good" or a "bad" husband in the past.

To some extent both of them were right in what they were saying. John would be different if Margaret were not so aggressive. Margaret would be different if John would be more attentive to her feelings. But both were wrong about how to approach this problem.

I told them they couldn't control the other person. They could only change themselves. And each had a part:

John was not attentive enough to Margaret's feelings. He needed to be more responsive. Margaret sometimes wasn't clear enough in expressing her feelings or insistent enough about John respecting them. She needed to be more explicit and assertive.

At first Margaret thought this analysis was unfair because she believed that she did tell John what she wanted and what bothered her. It was just that he didn't listen. But as we talked it became clear that she only *sometimes* told him what was bothering her. And often she was very indirect in making her needs known. She would drop hints or ask meekly.

"But what's the point?" she inquired with sincerity. "He doesn't pay attention anyway."

"Well," he answered, "because you always come on like a bulldozer."

"Even when I'm calm you don't pay attention to what I'm feeling. I was calm about us going out on Sunday mornings. You just don't care about anyone but yourself."

"Maybe because you're such a bitch."

"Listen," I said, "stop the name-calling and defensiveness. The two of you can do this at home without me. If you're here to work on your problems, you've got to look at your own contribution. You've got to work on yourselves."

"But I still feel stuck," Margaret said. "Even when I calmly tell John my feelings, he doesn't listen to me. He doesn't take me seriously. I don't know what to do. That's when I give up."

I told Margaret that if John is not a good listener, hitting him and threatening to have affairs would never change things for the better. It only gives him a valid excuse for pushing her away. I told Margaret that she needed to remain persistent in expressing her thoughts and feelings. Maybe he would listen. If she worked on her part of the problem, hopefully he would match her efforts and rise to the occasion. That would be his part of the deal. In any event, nothing is gained by losing her temper. If she controlled her temper and he remained unresponsive to her feelings, at least then she would know where she stands.

"You both have to change at the same time," I said. "John, you need to be more attentive to Margaret's feelings. And Margaret, you have to be clearer and less explosive about your needs. You also need to learn disciplined, loving ways to communicate your anger and frustration. You can't keep blowing up."

Each person would benefit from making a change, I told them. If one of them became unstuck, the other might follow.

Margaret agreed that hitting John and making threats about having an affair only made matters worse. She said she would be willing to work on being more disciplined and less volatile in expressing her feelings.

At this point John said he would listen more closely to what Margaret wanted. But he still sounded angry, and again said, "No one has ever hit me before."

I said that I was certain Margaret would be less aggressive if he would pay more attention to her.

As it turned out, John had already made up his mind about Margaret. Even though he agreed to pay more attention to her feelings and agreed to go to Sunday brunch with her the next weekend, his heart was not in the relationship. They were stuck, and John didn't want to get unstuck. He had fixed ideas about how he wanted things to be, and Margaret didn't measure up. They had not been together long. He had never really invested in the relationship and didn't want to work on his own part in the matter. He was waiting for Margaret to screw up again. She sensed his cold feelings and never could shake her hurt and angry feelings. When she lost her temper a few more times, he ended the marriage.

From our brief counseling sessions, Margaret learned a great deal about cooperative relationships and about assertiveness. It seemed that John learned very little.

CHAPTER
7

Locked Horns

At her first marriage counseling session, Marilyn talked about how lonely it felt being with her husband, Tom, for the past five years. Both of them previously had been married and eventually divorced. Marilyn was concerned that this marriage was not going to work, either. It was just the two of them at home. Marilyn's sixteen-year-old son was in a residential treatment center because of severe behavioral problems. Tom had two grown children.

At their second counseling session, Marilyn leveled serious complaints about what Tom had done during the previous week:

"It was the same old stuff. We were supposed to have breakfast together on Wednesday morning, and Tom forgot. We were going to have dinner together twice this week. So what does he do? He sets two places in front of the television set. I bring the plates in. He eats, watches TV, and ignores me. He doesn't love me. He doesn't know anything about intimacy. I'm a convenience or something; I don't know. I'm the only one who does anything to make us feel closer or more intimate. When it comes to getting his attention, he'd rather watch television than eat with me. This is nonsense."

"Yes," Tom said, in answer to a question of mine, "I want to be close to her. Yes, I want to talk. But whatever I do is never good enough. Marilyn complains all the time that I don't talk. Well, I think we talk a lot. She complains that I don't talk about the right things. She complains that I don't tell her about my day. I stopped telling her about my day because she said I was talking too much about myself. Then she complains that I don't talk enough. I can't win. She says I don't want to do things together. I often suggest we do things. I even suggested we visit friends this past weekend, but Marilyn didn't want to do that."

"Yeah," Marilyn said, "it's always with other people. You never want to do anything with just me. I'm your sidekick or something."

"You see," Tom said to me, "this is how she treats me. Nothing is ever good enough."

Tom and Marilyn's pattern of conflict is not unusual. In many relationships, one person—hurt about the lack of intimacy—chastises a partner for being deficient in the ability to love. When this happens, the partner—feeling criticized and hurt—has even less desire to be close. It just keeps getting worse.

LOCKED HORNS

"You two have your horns locked," I explained. "Each of you is very much bothered by what the other one is doing. Yet each of you is doing something that reinforces exactly what you don't like. It's a vicious circle.

"Tom, you hate it when Marilyn tells you that you're an unloving person. Yet you don't give her much attention. She's hurt by this. And when she's hurt, she gets critical and says that you're unloving. Then you pull back more. If you want her to stop describing you as unloving, you need to stop pulling back. You've got to show that you care.

"Marilyn, you say that you're hurt by Tom's distance. You say you want more closeness. Yet when you criticize him the way you do, you kind of chase him away. He told you that he—"

"Wait," Marilyn interrupted. "I can see I chase him away. But what am I supposed to do, just keep my mouth shut? I'm hurt that he doesn't want to spend any time with me. He's a cold fish. He only cares about himself. That hurts. It would hurt anyone."

"See," Tom said, "that's why I don't want to be close with her. Wouldn't you keep a distance if you were being hounded this way? This is what she does all the time."

I explained to them that they were doing *now* exactly what I had been talking about. Surely Marilyn wanted closeness. Surely she was hurt that there was not more closeness. But calling Tom a "cold fish" would not bring him closer.

Tom hated the name-calling. But he wasn't solving the problem by keeping a distance. In fact, he was making matters worse.

I explained that couples have *locked horns* when the styles of the two individuals clash and reinforce each other in a negative way. The clashing styles create a vicious circle. The more critical that Marilyn is, the more withdrawn Tom becomes. The more he withdraws, the more critical she becomes. If either one of them could break this pattern, they would still have a problem, but they wouldn't be locking horns. At that point they could possibly solve their problem.

At the time, Tom and Marilyn were locking horns in a dog-eat-dog competition. With all the criticism he took from Marilyn, Tom felt that she didn't like him. So he withdrew. With all the distance Tom put between himself and her, Marilyn felt he didn't love her. So she criticized. Each person held the line and wouldn't budge. Both of them were losing.

OTHER WAYS IN WHICH PEOPLE LOCK HORNS

To help them better understand the idea of locked horns, I gave several examples of the ways in which couples typically lock horns.

• *Attacking and Defensive Pattern.* In this pattern, one person criticizes and attacks the other. The one who is under attack feels threatened, puts up a defensive wall, and is unwilling to listen. The attacker is not being heard, so increases the intensity of the attack. This makes the other person even more defensive. They have locked horns.

• *Tuned Out and Hysterical.* In this pattern, one person (usually a woman) tells her feelings to a partner (usually a man), who discounts the feelings. He brushes them aside as trivial or silly. This makes her feel even more emotionally passionate. When she expresses her more intense feelings, he calls her "crazy" or "hysterical" for feeling the way she does. The more he discounts her feelings, the more passionate she becomes. They have locked horns.

• *Controlling and Passive-Resistant.* A takeover, controlling person makes the decisions. The other person is swept along but resents the dominance. The controlled person passively resists by sabotaging the agreed-upon plans. This makes the controlling person feel ever more compelled to be responsible and to take even more control of the situation. This angers the passive person, who becomes increasingly irresponsible about following through with the plans. They have locked horns.

• *Pushing and Withdrawing.* One person aggressively pushes for more closeness, scaring the other person, who withdraws. The more this person withdraws, the greater the need of the first person for closeness, and the greater the ensuing push. They have locked horns.

MUTUAL CHANGES

The best way for couples to unlock their horns is by both people making parallel changes at the same time. To break their vicious circle, Tom needed to be more nurturing. He needed to show more interest in Marilyn. Marilyn needed to stop being so harshly critical. She could express herself assertively, but without the put-downs. The more Marilyn felt loved, the less critical she would be. The less Tom was criticized, the more affection he would feel.

If they unlocked horns, Marilyn would feel loved. Tom would feel appreciated. Both of them would be happier.

THE OTHER GUY WON'T CHANGE

Marilyn listened to what I was saying, agreed it made sense, but then said, "The problem is that Tom will never change." This, by the way, is the major objection to making mutual changes: One person or both believes that the other one will not change. This objection slows people or prevents them from agreeing to make mutual changes. If the negativity persists, it also becomes a factor any time a partner slips or makes a mistake, as in, "See, just what I thought. He'll never change."

But this is an egocentric, mistrustful, one-sided outlook. The whole problem is attributed to the partner.

Marilyn explained what she expected would happen with Tom if both agreed to change: "He'll say he's going to do things differently. He'll say whatever you want him to say. He'll say whatever he thinks I want him to say. But he won't follow through. I will still be the only one who wants intimacy and seeks closeness—except for sex. He's always eager for that. It's just that he doesn't know how to get close on an emotional level."

"See what I mean?" Tom said, turning toward me.

"Look," I warned Marilyn, "you're back in your critical attitude. This chases Tom away. The whole idea is to change the system. Both of you change. I'm not saying that you have a guarantee that the other person will change. What I am saying is that this old system hasn't worked. You've complained and been critical of Tom, and demanded that he be more intimate for a long time, right?"

"Yes."

"Has it worked?"

"No, not really."

"That's my point. It hasn't worked the way you're doing it. And Tom, you've withdrawn under the barrage of criticism. But it doesn't stop the criticism from happening, does it?"

"No, not at all," he conceded.

What was especially important, I explained, was that they were only making matters worse by how they were responding to each other. They weren't just stuck, they were also digging an ever deeper hole for themselves. In a sense each of them was so focused on the other person's wrongdoing that neither could see the impact of his or her own behavior.

I told them that their dilemma reminded me of an episode from the television series *Cheers*. That episode involved Norm Peterson, a man who spends most of his time at a bar and almost none at home with his wife. He practically lived on his favorite barstool. When Norm heard that his wife might be having an affair, he retreated to the poolroom in the back of the bar and said to a friend, "I've been racking my brains trying to figure it out. Day after day, night after night, I sit on that stool out there trying to figure out why did she lose interest in me."

With these lines Norm illustrates how frightfully bad people can be at recognizing their own impact on other people. I told Tom and Marilyn that, like Norm Peterson, they needed to be more aware of the effect of their own behavior on each other.

Marilyn knew for sure that Tom would be distant if she put him down with severe criticism. However, she did not know what he would be like if she were less negative.

Tom knew for sure that Marilyn would criticize him if he were distant. However, he did not know if the criticism would subside if he were more attentive to her needs.

If they wanted to improve their relationship, both needed to agree to change together—to do their own part, and to trust that their partner would respond well.

If people don't trust that their partner will change, then they can never stop locking horns. And if they don't recognize that they have helped perpetuate the problem, they probably would not be capable of trusting their partners.

I told Tom and Marilyn that even in the worst possible outcome—you change and your partner doesn't—you still benefit from your own efforts: You get to feel good about yourself. You take away your partner's excuse for not doing better. And you really see where you stand with your partner—how he or she behaves under the best possible circumstances. I mentioned this outcome to them but didn't want to sound pessimistic. Rather, I stressed how good it would feel if each would make important changes together.

STUCK NEGOTIATION

For years I had been aware that couples lock horns, before I finally realized that this type of stalemate actually represents a peculiar power problem, a breakdown of negotiation. What happens with locked horns is that each person is trying to get what he or she wants by insisting that the partner do something different. Tom wanted Marilyn to stop being so critical. Marilyn wanted Tom to be closer and more intimate. He said what he wanted her to do. She said what she wanted him to do. The more each person insisted the other one should do all the changing, the deeper the problem became. Neither realized that the only way to solve the problem would be by concessions by both sides at the same time. To succeed would require a creative vision and a cooperative solution. Neither person could solve the problem alone. Both have to change, and neither is likely to change unless the other works on making simultaneous changes.

With a cooperative vision:

• Tom could realize that instead of telling Marilyn to stop criticizing him, he could give her what she wanted (intimacy) and see if maybe the criticism would subside.

• Marilyn could realize that instead of demanding intimacy and chastising Tom, she could make sure he understood what she wanted and calmly watch to see if he delivered.

People find it hard to think of these solutions because it requires a cooperative mentality. It requires confidence and competence in sharing power.

INTIMACY AND CRITICISM

As it became clear how Marilyn and Tom locked horns, I asked Tom what bothered him most. He said he was most troubled when Marilyn called him names like "cold fish." He hated that. He also hated that she implied he didn't love her when, in fact, he knew he did. Tom said she made him feel like such a failure, like he was inadequate. When he tried to give her what she wanted, she complained anyway.

I asked Marilyn what bothered her most. She said that Tom didn't seem to want closeness or value intimacy.

I reminded her that Tom had said he wanted more closeness in the relationship and that he felt frustrated in that his efforts seemed to fall short. I suggested that maybe the two of them needed to communicate better about what they meant by closeness and intimacy.

Over the following few weeks we had a very interesting discussion on the topic, beginning with a review of their childhood experiences. Neither Tom nor Marilyn had grown up in a close, loving family. Neither of them had positive role models. Bickering and angry resentment had been the norm in Marilyn's family. Everyone was critical and angry at each other. Interestingly enough, Marilyn was now angry at Tom and critical of him. Marilyn also remembered feeling that she was not loved as a child. She had to make "loud noises" to get anyone's attention. This, she realized, is how she now felt with Tom. Thus her feelings about being unloved and needing to make "loud noises" predated their relationship.

Tom's family didn't bicker as Marilyn's had, but had been quite the opposite, totally disengaged from one another. That's why it felt natural for Tom to be so remote and to keep such distance in their marriage.

In a way, both Marilyn and Tom were reliving their childhood experiences in their marriage. Neither of them had much understanding of what a loving relationship looked like. Although Marilyn knew she wanted more from the marriage, she was confused about how to make it happen.

Tom said that Marilyn and two previous counselors had convinced him that he was missing something in terms of emotional closeness, but conceded that he didn't seem to "get it." He had been trying to do what Marilyn and the counselors told him he should do to be close. That was to reveal his "deep feelings." But, he said, it was hard to do that when it felt like a demand or a performance. He said he kept feeling like a failure at the "intimacy game."

As we talked, it became clear that Tom had been introduced to formularized intimacy. He was told that to be intimate a person must express deep, hidden feelings and truths about oneself. Understandably he felt awkward, on the spot, and ingenuine when he unspontaneously tried to cough up what was expected. Also, when he tried to comply, Marilyn followed with criticism. So Tom started feeling hopeless and angry about the whole process. He came to think of intimacy as some sort of torturous experience.

Teaching intimacy through gimmicks such as expressing deep feelings misses the spirit of it. I wanted to give Tom and

Marilyn a little inspiration, and thought it might help to provide a broader perspective.

I explained that intimacy is the wonderful feeling of being close to someone, feeling connected. You enjoy being together; you love to do things together; you love to touch each other. When you have an intimate relationship, you're never alone against the world. There is always someone on your side who cares about you and wants you to feel good. By the same token, you derive great pleasure from satisfying your partner and making that person happy. You are stronger and happier together than you are when alone. You feel safe and protected. This, I explained, is why people want to open up completely with each other. Because they feel like a team. Because it feels good. *Not* because everyone tells you that you should be intimate. *Not* so you can do what you're "supposed to do."

As the discussion about intimacy continued, Tom realized that he had been trying to do what everyone expected of him. Instead of their following prescribed formulas, I suggested that both take time to think about what makes them feel close and happy together. Then they could get their own personal answers about intimacy, and work to incorporate them into their relationship. This began a dialogue that led to deeper self-understanding about emotional closeness and to a much better understanding of each other. Through this process of reflection and discussion, Marilyn was surprised to learn that Tom feels close when the two of them watch television together, side by side, or just sit in the same room, even if they aren't interacting. Tom learned that Marilyn feels most "loved" when he initiates some sort of activity together.

After a few weeks of discussing intimacy, Tom was much more excited about the whole idea. Intimacy no longer seemed to be a test at which he kept failing. Marilyn realized that her critical edge had been obstructing progress. So the two of them agreed to make mutual changes. Tom said he would act on his desire for greater closeness, thereby giving Marilyn the increased intimacy she wanted. At the same time, Marilyn said she would stop being so overly critical, and start looking for the positive qualities of her partner and of the relationship.

LAYERS AND LAYERS OF THE SAME THEME

With experience listening to couples, it becomes easy to identify the ways in which they lock horns. I can usually find the major contradictions in an hour session. Most couples are excited to discover the ways in which they have locked horns, in part because the truth is so evident once it is clearly explained. At last they understand a source of stress that had been such a mystery and caused such grief. This awareness gives a couple hope and is an important first step toward improvement in their relationship. But seeing the big picture is just the beginning. Next comes follow-through and making changes. The pattern of locked horns will reappear in a hundred different situations. A couple will have to uncover it over and over again in a variety of situations until they finally turn the corner and break free of its hold. To break the pattern, people must keep three keys ideas in mind:

1. They have to stay focused on their own individual part in locking horns—that is, they need to watch themselves vigilantly and follow through with changes. It is easy to revert unconsciously to old, familiar ways of behaving.

2. They should realize that their partner will not change overnight. They should expect that their partner sometimes will revert to old habits. These are the times when it is especially important not to slip into one's own old patterns. They would be locking horns again. Instead they should use careful, disciplined communication to tell their partner what they think is happening. Couples need to learn to constructively tell each other when they see problems. (The love stories in Chapter Eight demonstrate some ways to do this well.)

3. When a new conflict arises or an old one reappears, it should serve as a cue to look for the way in which they usually lock horns. Then each person needs to stay on track.

I told Marilyn and Tom that their changes would take time and would not come easily or swiftly. I warned that there would be setbacks. I said that Tom probably would be awkward at first in initiating intimacy. Marilyn probably would be critical at times. But if Tom didn't continue to make progress initiating closeness or if Marilyn became too critical, the process probably would stall.

As they continued to work on improving their marriage, they often locked horns in familiar ways. In each case, Marilyn was critical and Tom was trying to keep some distance. Here are four of the many problems they encountered as they were changing:

1. One week Marilyn complained that Tom got completely absorbed in his books at night. When he did this, he passively agreed with whatever Marilyn said without listening to her so she would be quiet. Marilyn called this behavior of ignoring her "antisocial."

Tom answered that getting married didn't mean that he could no longer read books. Anyway, he said, he was entitled to some private time. He further explained that growing up as one of seven children, he had learned to tune out extraneous noises and to concentrate while he was reading.

Tom was doggedly fighting to read, and telling Marilyn to leave him alone. Marilyn was hurt and accusing him of being antisocial. They locked horns in their customary way.

Here was a dilemma that required a cooperative solution. They needed new thinking. They had to find a way that would allow them closeness and also give Tom the freedom to read. Tom needed to realize that if he read all evening without paying attention to Marilyn, she would be hurt. Marilyn needed to allow Tom to have opportunities for undisturbed reading without calling him antisocial. When they recognized this and each avoided his or her negative tendencies (Tom to withdraw and

Marilyn to attack), they were able to negotiate a reasonable settlement.

2. When they planned weekends, Marilyn would push Tom to spend less time alone and with his friends, and more time together with her. Tom talked about all the activities he wanted to do alone. He felt threatened that he would lose his tennis, bowling, and good times watching the games with the guys. Marilyn was pushing for more togetherness. Tom was in a posture of fighting for his independence, fending her off.

At first, when Marilyn pushed hard to do something with Tom, he resented it, but would reluctantly concede. This never counted as shared time in Marilyn's mind because she had to push for it. It never really felt satisfying either because both were upset.

Marilyn would think, "If he really loved me, I wouldn't have to push so hard."

He would think, "I spend time with her, but it doesn't even count."

Because their negotiations about how to spend the weekends were causing them to lock horns, they saw that they needed to change gears. Although Marilyn had a right to ask for shared time, it became clear that she needed to ask assertively, without being so harshly critical. Also, she needed to allow Tom to have his independent fun without criticizing him. She made it clear that she supported Tom in having independent fun. For his part, Tom had to remind himself about his own commitment to closeness in the relationship. Bearing this in mind, he took more initiative in suggesting shared activities.

Breaking the pattern of locked horns (Tom withdrawing and Marilyn being critical), they were able to plan weekends that were satisfying to both of them.

3. Tom went on a business trip and didn't call to say where he was staying. Marilyn said, "If you loved me, you would never do anything like this. You're inconsiderate and selfish." Tom reacted by sarcastically implying that it was a relief to get away from her criticism, no matter where he stayed.

Once they realized how they had locked horns, Marilyn apologized for getting so extreme in her reaction. She said she should have expressed her hurt and resentment in more constructive ways. She knew she needed to give Tom room to make mistakes without attacking and saying that he was unloving.

Tom knew he had made a mistake by not calling home. He apologized for that and promised to be more careful in the future. He also apologized for the way he had angrily threatened to withdraw. Tom saw that it was important he not retreat when he felt threatened. In the future, if Marilyn ever put him down again, he needed to ask her assertively to stop instead of distancing himself from her.

4. A short time later, feeling bad because he had forgotten to call Marilyn on the business trip, Tom bought her flowers. Her reaction was critical: "You don't mean this. You're just doing it because you're supposed to."

Tom replied, "I give up. I don't want to be close with you. You're impossible to please."

Each was operating with negative assumptions about the other and therefore falling into old patterns. Marilyn assumed that Tom didn't want closeness. Tom assumed that Marilyn would be forever critical. Negative assumptions about a partner, such as these, are the big trap in making mutual changes.

In reviewing this fight, they realized that to move forward they needed to start with positive, not negative, assumptions: Marilyn needed to assume that Tom wanted more closeness, and accept that buying flowers was one of his ways to show it. Tom needed to assume that Marilyn was working on being less critical. He could think of the ways in which she had already changed. In this incident with the flowers, she made a mistake. Instead of backpedaling, Tom needed to allow for mistakes. He needed to be super-disciplined and couldn't let himself fall back into his own pattern of withdrawal.

MAKING PROGRESS

As they continued to talk about intimacy, they began to do more loving things for each other. Some of it was the typical "romantic" stuff, such as writing love notes and buying little gifts. Some of it was simply being more thoughtful of each other and helpful. For example: Tom offered to go out of his way to do some of the holiday shopping that Marilyn usually did in the past. Marilyn brought home soft drinks and chips for Tom so he could make a basketball game he was going to watch "more festive."

Soon the two of them began to have more fun together and to bend in terms of doing what the other preferred.

They began to feel more of a sense of coupleness—that is, they thought more as a team and more about each other. Their day-to-day happiness increasingly revolved around making each other happy. I don't want to make it sound as though this was a simple transition, because it was not. They faced numerous problems. But Marilyn and Tom eventually managed to break the cycle of locking horns. Tom didn't become Mr. Intimacy. Marilyn didn't totally lose her critical edge. But the two of them changed enough over time to substantially increase the quality of their life together.

CHAPTER

8

Loving Communication

When I asked Brian why he came to my office, he said because his wife might leave him.

I asked if she had issued an ultimatum.

"No, not that," Brian said, "but I'm afraid she'll jump ship, and I want to try to save our marriage."

He explained that his relationship with his wife, Julie, had been shaky from the beginning. They even broke up once for several months while they were still dating. Eventually they got back together, and in the bliss of a few nice days after their reunion, Julie laid out the ground rules: "We get married this time or it's over." And that's how it began.

Since the wedding day there had been much bickering over "just about anything," as Brian described it. It had been Brian who had threatened to leave for most of their five years together. But the tables turned recently. Julie had had enough of all the turmoil and threats, and finally said: "Yeah, you're right, let's end this." And she meant it.

I asked Brian if he thought Julie would come to counseling to work on their marriage.

"Ironically enough," Brian answered, "she was the one who wanted counseling all along. But now she's probably too angry at me to come."

This is a familiar scenario in my business. Often a person resists a partner's request to go for couple's counseling until a crisis explodes. By then the damage is serious. It's late, and sometimes too late, to save the relationship.

As Brian continued to describe their daily interactions, it was apparent that their relationship was in serious trouble. Both were intensely angry. They argued much of the time. On occasions they would yell and insult each other, sometimes using nasty language. Apparently Julie was fed up, and had one foot out the door.

"I know something you could do right away," I told Brian, "that could possibly make a dramatic improvement in your marriage. You could decide today—right here, right now—that you won't swear at Julie or insult her anymore. And also that you will stop yelling."

I explained that there are certain relationship basics, things you just cannot say or do to your partner if you want to build a loving relationship. Insulting, swearing, and yelling at each other are among the "no-nos" of communication.

I told Brian I knew it would be hard for him to make the change I had proposed because it involved breaking a habit. But, I assured him, it could be done. If he wanted to try to save the marriage at this point, it was going to require enormous effort.

He would start by telling Julie that he was going to stop swearing, yelling, and insulting her. He could say he hoped that she would make similar changes, or at least consider the possibility. Regardless of her response, he could and should stick to his own decision.

"If you truly want to work out relationship problems," I said, "you start by taking the high road: You do *your* end of things right."

Brian and I went back and forth on this proposal until he finally agreed it was a good idea and, in his words, "doable."

As we continued, he described the extraordinary amount of conflict in this relationship. I asked him why he wanted to stay with Julie. He said he must admit that part of the motivation was to avoid entering the dating scene all over again, including his fear of AIDS. But above and beyond the dating issue, he said he saw nice qualities in Julie and wanted to try to make a go of it. He also recognized and admitted some of his own problems, and expressed a willingness to work on them. He said that Julie's threat about leaving was a "wake-up call" that captured his attention.

COMMUNICATION SKILLS

To my surprise, Julie came with Brian to the next counseling session. She was impressed that Brian had taken the initiative to get help. She was also impressed that he had stopped yelling, swearing, and name-calling. He stuck to his guns.

Within a few minutes after we started the session, Julie directed the discussion to one of the major fights that had occurred during the past week. I suggested using a methodology that is often helpful to couples who need to improve communications. I asked them to report sentence for sentence—as close as they could recall—exactly what was said in their argument. This type of recall offers a couple a way to look at what happened, and a chance to consider what they could have done differently.

In this fight, Brian was angry that Julie was late for a date with some of their friends. They were going to meet at a nearby restaurant. Julie was still fixing her hair at the time they had planned to leave.

"You're too hung up on the way you look," Brian said. "You know appearances aren't everything. You're really overdoing it."

"I don't think I'm overdoing it," she answered. "I like to look nice. Actually, I think *you're* the one with the problem. You're not dressed right for tonight. Don't you realize we're going to a fancy restaurant?"

This was the beginning of a tense and unhappy evening for this couple.

In our session we realized that neither of them had been direct and honest with feelings. Brian was angry that Julie was late. Instead of directly saying so, he had said something critical about her being "too hung up" about her looks. Julie was hurt by his remarks. Instead of telling him that, she had said something hurtful in retaliation.

I decided to give them a quick example of how their interaction could have been better. I wanted to offer a sense of what is possible. I wanted to inspire hope, and make it clear that they could learn communication skills that would make a difference.

I told Brian that he could have said something like this:

"Julie, I'm annoyed that you're not ready on time for our date."

This would have been an honest expression of his feelings.

If he had expressed his annoyance in this manner, Julie could have apologized for being late, and offered the courtesy of saying when she would be ready. Also, she could have offered to call their friends if she was going to be more than a little bit late.

At that point, Brian would accept the apology, and the lateness matter would have been resolved.

Then came the issue of Brian's criticism of Julie. I asked him if he really believed that Julie "overdoes it on appearances," as he had said. He hedged a little, but then admitted that he did not. It was just a way to show his annoyance. Instead of being honest and direct, he was being provocative.

Next I asked Julie if she really felt Brian was underdressed for the evening, as she had said. Yes, she did think so. Did she tell him in a supportive way? I asked. No, she admitted, she had spoken in anger. I explained that offering helpful advice is one thing, but using criticism as ammunition in retaliation for being hurt is something entirely different.

Because the issue of criticism had arisen, I decided to talk more on that topic. I explained that some couples mistakenly believe that learning to communicate in loving ways means that they should stop being critical of one another.

"It would be sad if you stopped criticizing each other," I said with a smile.

"Well," Julie added, "I wouldn't want to stop now."

They both laughed, although somewhat nervously.

"Seriously," I explained, "you need the person you love to give you constructive criticism. If you're not being criticized, you're missing part of the truth of what your partner thinks. When you live with someone, you need the benefit of that person's observations. This includes observations about yourself and about the way you are with each other. The key word is *constructive*. The intent should be to support and build up your partner, not to tear each other down. When relationships are really clicking, partners help each other grow by offering constructive criticism.

And if the people we love can't help us grow and can't point out our shortcomings, who will? I like to make an analogy to an open pants zipper. Most people who notice an open zipper won't say a word. But if your partner won't tell you, who will? And don't you want to know the truth before you go out in public?

Constructive criticism, I added, must be offered with love, not malice. And there is an art to it. I told Brian and Julie we would be talking soon in more detail about constructive ways to give criticism and to handle other emotionally charged subjects.

Then I asked Brian, "If you two had not been arguing . . . if Julie hadn't been late . . . if Julie had asked nicely if you wanted her opinion about the way you were dressed for the dinner date . . . under these circumstances, would you have accepted her feedback?"

"Quite frankly," Brian answered, "given the way we get along—to be totally honest with you—I would have told her I'm not interested in her damn opinion . . . even though, as it turned out, she was right."

"That's too bad," I said. "You miss out on her feedback. And that's my point. The goal is for the two of you to have good communication so that you can be constructively supportive of each other, and stop these angry, hurtful, and mistrusting exchanges."

I reassured Brian and Julie that their communication difficulty was not unusual. Most people are not skilled at communicating what they think and feel in cooperative and loving ways. Whether it's hurt or angry feelings, or critical thoughts, few people have seen good role models. Most have seen examples of people hurting each other; either directly through vicious attacks, subtly and insidiously through indirect attacks, or unintentionally when feelings they have attempted to suppress suddenly erupt in destructive ways.

NEGATING A PARTNER

The way people communicate in our society reflects the general ways in which we are taught to act in relationships: competitively. We are either taught to make our own thoughts and feelings dominant, or to discount ourselves, including our thoughts and feelings, and to accept a subservient position. But we are not taught how to coordinate feelings, how to express them cooperatively and receive the feelings of others in that same spirit.

"Too often," I told Brian and Julie, "we are unable to see how two people can feel very differently about the same event, respect each other, and learn from the differences." I gave them an example to illustrate this point, involving a husband who was delayed at work and missed dinner with his family.

The wife said, "I'm angry you were late for dinner and didn't call."

The husband answered, "I was hurt that you and the kids didn't wait for me."

Both of their feelings were important. Each needed to hear the other. However, in this example, the wife rejected her husband's feelings: "How could we wait for dinner if you didn't call to let us know when you would be coming?"

Similarly, the husband stonewalled his wife: "Well, you know if I'm going to be more than an hour late, I would have called. I always do."

This was followed by a minor war of words, each of them discounting the other's position and defending his or her own.

I call this process *negating,* when one person ignores, dismisses, or brushes aside the feelings or opinions of the other person. By negating the other person, he attempts to make his own point of view dominant.

Sometimes people negate each other in an openly competitive spirit, in an effort to win. More often they do it automatically, without realizing it. People are so absorbed in their own point of view that they have trouble putting themselves in their partner's frame of reference.

I explained a basic principle to Brian and Julie: *Cooperative resolution to conflict begins when each person takes the other person's feelings seriously.*

In a cooperative relationship, a partner's feelings should not be seen as antagonistic. It is not a matter of one person's feelings being more important than another's. Consideration of both people's feelings provides valuable information about how the two individuals can coordinate their needs.

The husband and wife in the dinner dispute needed to take each other's feelings seriously. The wife had to recognize that her husband placed a high value on dinner with the family. The husband had to realize that his wife valued a phone call when he was going to be late for dinner. With this knowledge they could make agreements about the future.

For example, they could make this kind of a deal: If the husband was going to be more than half an hour late, he would call home. If he forgot to call or couldn't call, the family would begin dinner without him, after waiting for half an hour.

DISTORTIONS AND MISINTERPRETATIONS

To broaden Brian and Julie's understanding of communication, I described another way in which discussions become competitive. This happens when opinions or feelings that are expressed in a cooperative spirit are distorted or misinterpreted by the listener. I gave Brian and Julie a few of examples:

- During dinner a guy says he likes the vegetables. His wife answers, "You mean you don't like the meat."
- A woman states her preference about vacation plans. Her husband accuses her of trying to control their relationship.
- A wife tells her husband that her feelings were hurt when they didn't go out on a planned date. The husband calls this an attack on his character.

Too often people read more into communication than the person who spoke intended to say. Reasonable communication is sometimes misconstrued as put-downs, power plays, and attacks on character.

I was going to explain in greater detail when Julie started speaking:

"That's what happens with us," she said. "Every time I tell Brian that something is bothering me, he considers it an attack on his character. He gets *really* defensive about it and calls me a nag. I can't tell him that anything is bothering me without him turning it around and calling me a nag."

"It seems that everything bothers Julie," Brian replied. "She's always putting me down. In fact, I'm worried that these new communication techniques will only encourage her to be even more upset and critical than she is right now.

"She uses her feelings as a battering ram. Once she is upset, she won't relent. She nags endlessly with her complaints. Last week it was the roof repair. Before that, she complained that I don't send flowers or call her at work like I used to. She just doesn't let up."

Julie asked, "What am I supposed to do, just remain silent about everything that bothers me? All I do is tell you my feelings. Then you say I'm attacking you. You get defensive and call me a nag. I can't tell you what I feel, or ask you for anything, or say anything without you calling me a nag."

Then she turned toward me: "He feels attacked by what I say. He always tells me 'You hit me on the head with your feelings.' All I do is tell him what I feel. If he would only listen..."

They were in an attack/counterattack mode. I told them that this type of blaming is not in the spirit of cooperation. They needed to get back on track by examining their own behavior rather than pointing their fingers at each other.

Julie conceded that sometimes she did use put-downs, and that she needed to learn better ways to express her feelings. Brian admitted he had trouble accepting Julie's hurt and angry feelings, no matter how carefully they were presented, and that he tended to change the subject by calling her a nag. He also admitted that he sometimes automatically labeled her requests for anything as nagging.

CONFLICT-FREE RELATIONSHIPS

Part of the problem between these two people was that Brian visualized a relationship without conflict. When he was a child, he often witnessed his parents attacking each other. He did not have a role model of a couple lovingly talking out their differences. Seeing no mechanism for openly and constructively resolving conflict, he had decided to suppress his feelings, hoping to eliminate hostility and conflict.

When I started to explain that a conflict-free relationship is impossible, Julie interrupted, and said to Brian:

"You're big on calling me the troublemaker. You say I start all the conflict. The thing is, I bring our differences into the open. That gives us a chance to work them out. You don't *openly* show your feelings like I do. But you get just as angry. You show your gripes. You show them in passive ways. You show your anger by withdrawing. Sometimes you don't talk to me for several days. I hate that.

"And then," she continued, "you get so critical, like about my parents visiting. If I just mention that I disagree with your opinion about something, you call me a nag or a troublemaker. You want no conflict, *and* you want to control everything. You want me to quietly accept everything you do."

"Well," Brian said, "you *do* complain a lot. You're a griper."

"Listen," Julie replied, "you called me a griper the other day when my friends came to our table in the restaurant. You weren't even civil to them. You just sat there with a stone-cold face. You were rude to them and to me. It was hostile. When I said so, you called me a nag. Well, treat me right and I won't nag. And don't kid yourself. You're not above conflict. It's just that you express your hostility by withdrawing. I'm fed up with your selfish, controlling attitude. You want everything your way. You're not happy unless you're in control. You want to control me and my life."

In the beginning of her comments, Julie had been doing a pretty good job of critiquing Brian's attempt to suppress differences, and the way his feelings surfaced. However, toward the end, she started attacking his character and accusing him of deliberately and selfishly trying to control her life.

The attack mode was the model of conflict resolution that Julie had experienced in her family as a child. Differences were not suppressed. Conflict was openly expressed—but without much discipline. Eventually discussions would turn into donnybrooks.

It was hard to keep Brian and Julie from bickering. Their relationship was like a tinderbox, ready to ignite. They locked horns: Julie said what she felt, sometimes offensively and insultingly. Brian sometimes countered with insults, but mainly by withdrawing and calling her a nag. The more Brian wanted to avoid conflict, the more confrontational Julie became. The more confrontational she was, the more Brian wanted to avoid it. He would even threaten to leave the marriage. After five years of this, it was Julie who finally got serious about leaving.

As the session progressed, I told Brian that conflict is part of every relationship, and that couples need to learn to accept this and to communicate their thoughts and feelings. People who love each other, even the most loving of couples with the best of intentions, sometimes do things that hurt, annoy, frustrate, or otherwise upset their partners. They also have differences of opinion. But, I stressed to Brian and Julie, couples who want to take care of each other must communicate in disciplined, non-threatening ways. And they need to listen without getting defensive. Brian and Julie both needed help in learning cooperative communication techniques. We would talk about this next time.

STROKES

On several occasions during their first session together, I talked about the inevitability of conflict in relationships. As the session was winding down, I decided to try to end on a positive note. I explained that the ability of couples to sustain their efforts in resolving conflict is, to a large extent, a function of the amount of love and affection they express to each other on a daily basis. There has to be a reward for all the effort. That reward is the feeling of love, closeness, and intimacy.

Judging by the way they were fighting, it seemed likely that there wasn't much affection being expressed in this relationship. Brian and Julie confirmed my impression. They told me that they rarely said a positive word to each other anymore, and that their physical expression of love was practically nil.

Part of changing, I explained, would involve getting the positive flow of affection reestablished. I could see the urgent need for this if they wanted to save their marriage. So I asked at the end of the session for them to take a little time to say some nice things to each other. I tried to prompt them: I said they could say anything they liked about the other person, or anything the other person had done in the past that they appreciated. I said, "Even if you're very angry at each other from *before* today's session, you can at least say some nice things about the effort that was put forth today."

Often people find this task a little embarrassing, especially to be asked to do this in a counseling session, in front of a psychologist. But I presented the task as a necessary step toward learning to exchange affection.

Some couples can readily express affection. With coaxing, most couples eventually can say some sweet things to each other. But Brian, and especially Julie, could barely muster a friendly word.

I reminded them of the importance of starting a positive flow. I urged them to think of when they first met, and to talk about the initial attraction. Finally, with great prompting, Brian complimented Julie on "being willing to come to counseling to work on their marriage." He loosened up a little more, and told her he thought she was beautiful and also energetic. All Julie could say was, "You're a good, hard worker." The feeling was not there. Brian's difficulty in expressing kind words and Julie's lack of affection made for a poor prognosis. It was clear this relationship was in jeopardy. I told them both, but especially Julie, that their difficulty in expressing affection meant that this was more of a crisis than they might realize. It would be important to deal with negative feelings, presumably hurt and resentful ones, that were blocking the flow of affection.

PURPOSE OF COMMUNICATION: LOVING SPIRIT

At our next session, before teaching communication skills, I wanted to introduce Brian and Julie to the Basic Cooperative Agreement (BCA) and the super decision. It is only within the context of agreeing to cooperate with a partner and wanting to monitor oneself for proper behavior that communication becomes what I call *loving communication*. I told them that loving communication is always directed toward promoting love, support, understanding, and mutual well-being. Brian and Julie had been somewhat prepared for this: At Brian's first session I talked about the "no-nos" of communication: swearing, yelling, and insulting. At their first session together I had told them that criticism is important but that the intention must be to bring each other up, not to put each other down. Also I had told them that conflict can be handled cooperatively.

I explained that I've seen communication techniques abused, wherein one person tries to get more skilled at them than the other, to gain the upper hand. Word bullies use communication skills to compete. To prevent this, loving communication requires a commitment to cooperate.

People who practice loving communication are careful about the way in which they present their thoughts and feelings. I told Brian and Julie that when people agree to cooperate—when they make the super decision and a Basic Cooperative Agreement —certain important assumptions about communication follow:

• *They will make every effort to communicate their positive, loving, and supportive feelings.*

• *No one will deliberately hurt anyone else.* Some hurt is unavoidable; some is not. The BCA and the super decision ensure that we commit to minimizing unnecessary hurt and to learning from our mistakes to prevent unnecessary hurt in the future.

• *Each person will be committed to listening carefully to the other.* This is the only way to make sure that feelings are respected, differences of opinion are heard, and conflict is resolved cooperatively.

• *Each person will want to know when he has hurt or otherwise upset his partner, and when his partner is feeling bad about something.* Couples with a BCA are committed to each other's happiness. To be responsive, they need to know what their partners feel.

• *Couples will commit to bringing conflict into the open so it can be handled in direct and sensitive ways and settled to everybody's satisfaction.* If conflict does not come out, it cannot be addressed. Therefore it must be brought forth.

• *Couples will be careful, sensitive, and disciplined in communication. They will speak with respect and without aggressiveness.* When conflict erupts in threatening and abusive ways, it diminishes goodwill and reduces the likelihood of arriving at a cooperative solution. With a BCA, people do not need to be aggressive because their partners pay attention and work hard at listening to what is being said, without getting defensive.

• *No one will deliberately use aggressive or manipulative communication methods to try to dominate.* No one will give *away personal power and accept a subordinate role.* A BCA means that couples agree to overcome tendencies to dominate or submit, and to work toward an ideal of equality and cooperation.

Julie quickly responded to my introduction about cooperative communication by saying that Brian broke the rules all the time. He didn't listen. In the past couple of weeks he had stopped swearing and yelling, but his quiet withdrawal was getting worse. He wasn't listening. Then she offered an example. During one of these weeks she had told Brian how she felt about a social evening with some friends. While she talked, he sat there impassively, and then, in Julie's words, "ignored everything I said and walked off."

"No," Brian answered, "you launched one of your typical attacks. I was listening, but I refused to get hooked. I heard everything you said. That's why I left the living room and went back to the bedroom to read."

Apparently Julie had listed several complaints about Brian's participation at a party that they had attended on Saturday night. During the counseling session they were able to reconstruct Julie's comments:

- You get too quiet and too withdrawn when we socialize.
- At the party you seemed preoccupied in your own thoughts, and that was rude to our hosts.
- Too often you leave all the burden of carrying the conversation on me.

"Well," Julie said to Brian after we clarified her complaints, "what's wrong with these statements? Everything I said is true. I didn't invent this stuff to make you feel bad."

Brian had an answer. He was quick with new knowledge. He said:

"You're trying to use communication to dominate me. That's not cooperative. You're telling me how I should behave at parties."

"I'm just telling you what I think," Julie replied.

"Yeah, like the commissar of truth," Brian said. "I don't have to be as outgoing as you are. And it's your choice, not mine, to take so much responsibility in social situations. Anyway, you care more about the well-being of the Schneiders [their hosts] than about me. I was upset Saturday night. But you didn't give a damn about *that*."

There was certainly validity to each person's criticism: Julie had stated her feelings and opinions as if they were indisputable truths, not merely her own point of view. Brian had left the room instead of responding to what had been said, and only now was talking about it.

But there was a bigger issue: Clearly the two of them had not really accepted the Basic Cooperative Agreement. They were still eagerly trying to punch holes in each other's armor.

I explained that it was senseless to critique each other's lack of cooperativeness until they really decided to cooperate.

"Look at the way you two bicker. You're going to have to change your attitudes if you want to make this relationship work. You need to decide if you want to cooperate. If you choose to bicker like this, there's nothing I can do. I'm not a judge who will declare a winner. You'll be wasting your time and money, and my time, if you come here to slug it out. This competitive bickering is a serious problem. If you want to keep coming to see me, you need to decide to change."

At this point they weakly agreed to cooperate. I told them I was not totally convinced that they had committed to cooperate, but that we could go ahead and revisit the agreement later.

SAYING WHAT YOU THINK

As I had promised the week before, I wanted to give Brian and Julie guidelines for cooperative ways of handling emotionally charged communication. I wanted to introduce them to loving communication as it applies to upset feelings, disagreements, and criticism.

I started by telling them about a problem that seemed relevant to their situation: egocentrism. Egocentrism means the world centers on oneself. You see things from your own eyes, but not the eyes of others. Egocentric communication is one of the major obstacles to loving communication. People who communicate egocentrically send the following types of messages:
- This is what I feel. (It is the only way to look at what's happening.)
- This is what I think. (Therefore, this is the way it is.)
- My point of view is the absolute truth. (It is the only valid way to see things and all that matters.)

An excellent way to counter an egocentric tendency is to learn to speak with a degree of humility—in unassuming ways—using phrases such as these:
- "This is my opinion . . . "
- "This is what I think . . . "
- "These are my feelings . . . "
- "It appears to me . . . "

This type of phrasing allows for another person's point of view.

This is not wimpiness. You can have strong feelings and opinions. You can be self-assured about your own judgments. But you must not insist that you have a corner on the truth, or on "rightness." Too often people overcommit to their own way of thinking.

It is also important always to ask what your partner is thinking or feeling. It is a good idea, in fact, either to precede your statements, or follow them, with a question such as:
- "What do you think?"
- "What is your opinion?"
- "How do you feel about this?"

There has to be room for differences. The idea of loving communication is that all individuals say what they think and feel, so that everything is out in the open. Then negotiations can begin. "You have to keep an open mind," I said. "Your partner's feelings need to be taken seriously, even if they seem to conflict with your own."

The danger is self-certainty, in which an individual is convinced that his or her own point of view is right, even if the partner disagrees. If everybody is self-certain, there is no dialogue. Nobody is willing to shift opinions.

ASKING PERMISSION

In the spirit of cooperation, I told Brian and Julie, it's essential that listeners are as interested in receiving a message as speakers are in sending it. This means that timing is important, and that speakers should be sure that listeners are receptive. The best way to do that is by asking for permission to proceed.

Sometimes people are not in the right mood to listen; perhaps they are too busy or preoccupied. Sometimes they simply do not want anyone's input at a particular moment or regarding a particular issue.

Too often speakers plunge ahead with feedback without preparing a partner for the impact of what is said. Then couples attempt to deal with emotionally charged communication when they are not in the right frame of mind. It is better to find times to talk when both people are in the right mood.

In asking permission to proceed, it's best you give some indication about what you will be saying. For example:
- "I'd like to talk with you about something that upset me last night. Can I tell you now?"
- "Something you did while my mother was here annoyed me. Can I tell you about it?"
- "I would like to settle our differences about summer vacation. Can we talk about it?"
- "I have some advice about your work situation. Would you like to hear it?"

Asking permission to proceed gives the potential recipient a chance to determine if he or she is ready and willing. If he or she is receptive at that moment, it gives that person a chance to prepare mentally for the communication that will follow. It makes the emotional impact of the statement less sudden.

If the listener is not receptive at that moment, the cooperative response is to suggest another time in the near future:
- "I'm too busy right now. Can we talk in about an hour?"
- "I'm upset about something this evening. Could we talk about what's on your mind tomorrow morning?"

One way or another, time must be found to talk. Timing should not be used as an excuse to avoid discussions indefinitely.

CONSTRUCTIVE CRITICISM

In relationships, criticism is one form of saying what you think. Some of what you think about a partner and his or her behavior is critical. If handled well, these opinions constitute constructive criticism. Because Brian and Julie had no vision, parameters, or guidelines for giving criticism, time and again they had brutalized each other with their words.

Most people, like Brian and Julie, are trained to handle criticism competitively. Too often it is used as a weapon in a power struggle. Too often it is egocentric and offered as "absolute truth," when really it is only one person's opinion. Too often people do not have the sensitivity to give criticism in a way that feels supportive. Too often what could be helpful advice is given with an angry tone of voice. Too often people start with angry confrontations, either because they assume the listener will be defensive, or because they want their own thinking to prevail.

I explained that in loving communication, the intent of criticism is to support and build up a partner and to enhance a loving relationship. Criticism should be presented in a manner consistent with the intent.

In fairness, all criticism always should be viewed as one person's opinion—that is, the way one person sees things. Someone else, including your partner, may see things differently. Your job is not to win a struggle for the dominance of your ideas. Rather, the point is to say what you think and to offer an opportunity for your partner to listen. If there is disagreement, couples must learn to have a loving dialogue to resolve the difference.

I gave Brian and Julie a few general rules of thumb for constructive criticism:

- The tone of voice should be loving, calm, and reasonable.

- Never present criticism in an attempt to impose your will on a partner; to this end, avoid name-calling or put-downs. Stay away from extreme terms such as "always" and "never" unless they are completely accurate descriptions of what you are saying. Don't keep repeating yourself.

- Be as specific as possible, so that a partner knows what you are talking about. If you make generalizations, give some specifics.

This is an example of a general statement:

"You are slow to get around to the household projects that you say you are going to do."

These are the specific examples:

"You said you would finish the roof repair last month but haven't done it yet. You said you would bring the car in this past week but didn't do it. And you told me you were going to water the plants yesterday. You didn't do it."

- Be sure to distinguish fact from opinion.

A fact would be: "I've noticed that you don't finish some of your projects, such as the roof repair, when you say you will."

An opinion would be: "In my opinion, you set unrealistic deadlines."

Julie listened with interest to the guidelines for constructive criticism. Then she asked a very important question: "Let's say we get everything into the open but don't agree about any of it. Then what happens?

"I'm sure," she continued, "Brian will try to build a case that I'm a nag and that I want to control his life."

I told Julie that she was making a negative assumption about Brian. I reminded her of the Basic Cooperative Agreement. If she wanted a cooperative relationship, she needed to behave differently and trust that Brian would do the same. Negative assumptions sabotage progress.

"Sure," I told her, "it's a leap of faith to try it. But you came here to do things differently. If you keep mistrusting and doubting each other, nothing will change. You are unhappy with the status quo. So think about making a serious effort based on a cooperative agreement."

I continued, "Your question, Julie, about differences of opinion is important. First, I can reassure you, many differences are cleared up once people learn to talk cooperatively with each other. Just getting them into the open often clears the air. Then comes negotiation. Couples have to learn to settle their remaining differences through loving and cooperative negotiation. I'll be showing you those skills soon. But before you can begin to negotiate, the two of you need to learn to get your issues into the open, or we could say, onto the negotiation table. That's part of what good communication is all about."

The two of them seemed to mellow somewhat. By the end of the session, neither Brian nor Julie was jumping at the other. There were inklings of goodwill.

FORMAT FOR UPSET FEELINGS

At the next session, we continued the discussion about loving communication, with a special focus on communicating upset feelings. Neither of them started with a clue about how to do this cooperatively. They only knew competitive ways to deal with feelings. Like most people, they either submissively discounted their feelings or competitively imposed them on others. They had never had role models who communicated cooperatively, in careful and disciplined ways. Most people, like Brian and Julie, need guidance about how to communicate upset feelings.

I introduced them to a format I recommend for expressing hurt, sad, angry, or any other upset feelings. It is a fill-in-the-blanks sentence that goes like this:

"When you did (A), I felt (B)."

In this format, (A) is a description of a specific behavior, such as, "When you left dirty dishes in the sink after dinner" or "When you said I was lazy." In describing the behavior, it is important to be specific. For example, it is better to say, "When you left crumbs on the kitchen counter and dishes in the sink" than the more general, "When you left a mess in the kitchen." The more specific the speaker is in explaining the behavior, the better the chances are that the listener will understand the event being described.

In this format, (B) is a description of how you feel now or felt at the time, such as angry, annoyed, hurt, sad, or scared.

A complete sentence using this format would be, "When you left dirty dishes in the sink after dinner last night, I felt resentful." Another example would be, "When you said I was lazy, I felt frightened and angry."

The beauty of this format is that people get to say how they felt when a specific event occurred. Assuming that the event is not fictional, this statement becomes an indisputable expression of emotion, saying essentially, "When (A) happened, this (B) is how I felt." People who love each other want to know how they are affecting their partners.

If your partner is upset or angry, it doesn't necessarily mean you should stop what you're doing, although you might. But at a minimum, you should take the feelings seriously and think about the impact of your behavior on your partner.

I went into detail in explaining this format for Julie and Brian. They seemed to recognize its merit and agreed to begin using it. I warned them that everyone makes mistakes during the learning process. I also assured them that if they would be patient, they would find this format most helpful in settling differences.

Next Brian, Julie, and I discussed how to receive an upset feeling expressed in this format. I said the best way is to listen carefully, and to acknowledge hearing what was said. Usually no other response is required. People simply need to know that their feelings are being heard. That's all it takes. Sometimes listeners will want to respond. It is best to wait—to think about what was said—especially if the response is in any way defensive.

I then suggested that Brian and Julie try this format with each other.

Julie wasted no time in putting the theory to practice. She did a good job of expressing a resentment: "When you called me stupid in front of my friends at the Mexican restaurant last week, I was hurt and embarrassed and angry."

"Well," Brian answered quickly and defensively, "it *was stupid* that you waited so long to speak to your boss about your schedule. That's why I called you stupid."

We needed to talk more about better listening.

LISTENING WITHOUT GETTING DEFENSIVE

Using what had just transpired as an example, I explained to Brian and Julie that the most important part of listening was to take seriously whatever was said. The listener must make an effort *not* to disregard or discount the speaker's feeling or opinion.

I warned that there is a competitive tendency to answer back, to get defensive, or to counterattack. We see other people's feelings or opinions as antagonistic. We feel threatened and worry that the other person wants to dominate. So we try to dismiss the other person. We try to make our own feelings and opinions prevail.

Competitive training teaches people to think these thoughts:

"If I listen, I lose."

"If I listen to what my partner wants, I have to do things his (or her) way."

"If I listen to criticism, I must accept it as true."

I recommended that Brian and Julie take an inventory of their listening skills. Some indicators of poor listening include: interrupting a partner who is speaking; answering what was said without taking time to think about it; a rebuttal attitude of disagreeing and dissecting whatever is said; thinking of what you will say while the other person is speaking; and changing the topic, sometimes tit-for-tat (e.g., "I'm angry about the amount of money you spent on clothing" is answered with "Well, I'm angry that you spent so much money last Christmas"). Other indicators of poor listening are distortions and misinterpretations, which Brian, Julie, and I had talked about two weeks earlier.

Both Brian and Julie acknowledged that they were poor listeners. I suggested they begin the practice of pausing before they responded—to reduce defensiveness. Then they needed to look for what is right in what the other person is saying. One way to think about it, I told them, is to put yourself in your partner's shoes. Also, it always helps to remind yourself of the purpose of loving communication within the context of a Basic Cooperative Agreement: "I am building a loving, cooperative relationship. I don't give up power by listening, because no one is trying to dominate me. I can even listen to strong feelings and strong criticism without being threatened and without losing anything. I will gain understanding. Even if I don't like what is being said, and don't agree, I will better understand my partner's point of view. That will help us reconcile our differences. I will have an opportunity to speak later."

Brian, Julie, and I went back to Julie's resentment about being called stupid, and Brian's response to it. Brian acknowledged his defensiveness and apologized. It seemed like important progress. But Julie remained angry and said, "He's so defensive. That's why I feel so hopeless about things."

NO-BICKERING DECISION

From the start it was clear that bickering was a serious problem with Brian and Julie. I told them that in some ways their bickering habit was like a serious drinking habit. They started fights the way an alcoholic would reach for alcohol. It was almost automatic. And I said a bickering habit such as theirs can only be stopped the way a drinking habit is stopped: by the use of a huge amount of willpower. "If you want to stop bickering, it's going to require enormous concentration and effort. You have to decide to stop.

"Every week," I told them, "I notice that each of you tells me what the other person is doing wrong. I'm not a referee or a judge. My job is to help you stop these fights, not to proclaim a winner. The only way you win is if you *both* win. If you both want to stop these fights, you have a chance. But you need to be serious about your cooperative agreement. You have to change your ideas about the relationship. Your relationship will not be fixed by pinning responsibility on your partner. It will be fixed only if you do your part differently. You have to decide if you want to change."

Their arguing had a distinctive quality. Julie was generally first off the starter block. It went all the way back to their wedding. She was the one who said, "We get married this time or it's over." At her first session with Brian, it was she who brought up the first problem. When I taught the technique for expressing emotionally charged issues, she was quick to share a resentment. Her expressiveness was important, but by always going first, she grabbed the initiative. Brian's tendency was to withdraw. So I suggested that Brian work hard on coming forth with his feelings and initiating discussions. I suggested that Julie should allow room for that, and when she was eager to talk, might consider asking Brian about his thoughts and feelings before she offered hers.

Brian seemed interested and made an effort over the next few weeks to apply some of the methods and techniques we had discussed. Consistent with what Brian had said in our first session, Julie seemed less interested in saving the marriage. She seemed to like the communication techniques, and put them to use, especially in getting out her accumulated anger. In this regard she was relentless. But she did not seem fully committed to the cooperative spirit. Brian wavered in his commitment.

Soon Brian started saying that he didn't think Julie wanted to save the relationship. He put it this way:

"You never wanted to hear my opinions. You have always wanted to run things. Now that I'm doing better at saying what I think and feel, you want out . . . because you can't control me anymore. It feels like you're on the warpath."

In this statement, Brian expressed his theory—his suspicion—as if it were an absolute truth. This couple needed to learn another important concept in loving communication: how to communicate and respond to suspicions.

SUSPICIONS

Even with superb communication, I told Brian and Julie, a couple cannot know all the details of each other's lives. At times we may detect something that a partner is thinking, feeling, or doing, but not fully understand it. So we fill in the gaps of communication with our imagination. Sometimes we imagine wonderful things. Sometimes we are suspicious and suspect negative things. Because suspicions are a totally normal part of loving relationships, couples need a mechanism for checking them out.

In our counseling session, Brian had just expressed a couple of suspicions rolled into one. He suspected that:
1. Julie didn't want him to say his thoughts and feelings.
2. Julie didn't want to be in the relationship anymore because he was now saying what he thought and felt.

I told Brian and Julie that most people make either of two mistakes with suspicions:
1. They assume their suspicions are totally true. (If I think it's so, it must be so.)
2. They brush aside their suspicions, assuming they must be wrong. (I'm silly to think this way.)

Assuming suspicions are true tends to stir up conflict. Assuming they are wrong leaves people unsettled, without an adequate explanation for what they sense. Brushed aside, suspicions tend to persist and become more intense and elaborate.

Almost always, a suspicion has a grain of truth. People have detected something but cannot quite explain it.

The cooperative way to handle suspicions about a partner is neither to assume that they are correct nor that they are wrong. Rather, you test them out. You put suspicions forth tentatively and seek validation. Then it is the listener's responsibility to find at least a grain of truth, something that may have triggered the suspicion.

The premise is cooperation. The premise is a commitment to promoting understanding. So when people check out a suspicion, their partners will help them find the validity of it. In a sense, partners communicate this message: "I take your suspicion seriously. I want to help explain it and alleviate your uneasiness. I want to help you account for your feelings." Sometimes suspicions are absolutely correct. Sometimes they are only partially correct. For example, one of the most common suspicions in friendship and love relationships is that the other person wants to "break up" or "doesn't like me anymore." Very often this is not exactly true, but the grain of truth is that the person is angry or upset about something and has not discussed it.

Often people have trouble validating the suspicions of people they love. Sometimes they even have trouble recognizing the truth within themselves. If they can't admit the truth to themselves, it will be impossible to communicate to their partner. Nevertheless, couples who want good communication must learn to express their suspicions and to validate their partner's suspicions. On the positive side, the need to give validation—to find what is true about a partner's suspicion—often stretches one's perseverance at looking for one's own hidden motivations and feelings.

Brian agreed to check out his suspicions. He turned to Julie and said:

"Well, I'm suspicious that you can't stand that I'm more assertive about expressing my feelings."

"Look, Brian," Julie answered, "I've been after you since we met to express your feelings. I'm not at all upset you're expressing them assertively now."

But Julie did not offer any validation for Brian. I urged her to think twice: Was she glad that Brian was saying his feelings? Was there anything about him saying his feelings or the way he was saying them that displeased her? If not, what was making him suspicious?

Julie remained defensive: "Well, I think he is just uncomfortable saying what he feels. He has always been uncomfortable with it. So he's projecting his discomfort on me."

Again I reminded Julie that her job was to validate Brian, not to discount him. Then came a difficult truth, directed to Brian:

"I guess I have to admit," Julie said, "I'm not really sure I want to hear your feelings at this point. I'm so mad at you for all the times you wouldn't talk with me, and all the times you threatened to leave. It seems like it's too late."

Well, then, there was a large element of truth in Brian's suspicion. I empathized with Julie about her long-term distress, and helped Brian deal with the pain of Julie's apparent rejection. Eventually I pointed to the dilemma: If Julie wanted to go forward, she must be forgiving, accept her 50 percent share of the responsibility for what had gone wrong, and work through her rage. It would be hard for Brian to maintain a cooperative attitude for a prolonged time if Julie remained continually angry at him.

And this led to the second part of Brian's suspicion, which he brought forth again: that Julie didn't want to be with him anymore.

Julie started out defensively but, when pressed to find the validity in Brian's suspicion, admitted that she was quite uncertain about continuing with the relationship. It didn't surprise me, given how uncooperative and angry she had been. Brian was shocked and started pushing for more information. Julie didn't want to talk. She clammed up. We were too close to what was going on inside her. There was little we could do at this time except to help Brian cope with the pain and to encourage Julie to clarify where she stood. The session ended.

The next night, Brian called me at home. Julie had just admitted that she was having an affair with another guy. She said she had begun liking the guy before Brian came for help and had been sleeping with him since precisely the week he had come alone for the first appointment.

People are intuitive. Brian was right to suspect that Julie wanted out of the relationship. He thought it was because he had become assertive. Rather, it was because they had fought for too long before they began to do anything about their problems. The flow of emotional and physical affection between them had stopped. Julie had given up, gone elsewhere to meet her needs, and started a relationship with another man. Brian and Julie separated and were divorced shortly after this revelation.

From practical experience, the two of them had discovered the power of learning to trust, test, and validate suspicions: With this type of communication, the truth comes out. If couples love each other and want to cooperate, they can go far with the truth. If they are antagonistic, the truth will help them go apart.

At this point it was all speculative as to why Julie had come to counseling in the first place. Probably part of the motivation was because she held some hope about the relationship, part because she was unsure of herself, part because she felt guilty about what she was doing, and part because it was a chance to let out her anger at Brian. The affair did seem to explain her apparent reluctance really to accept the Basic Cooperative Agreement. Despite the sad ending of the relationship, I believe that Julie gained some understanding of the type of communication that is possible in a loving, cooperative relationship.

I know that Brian learned much about cooperation and communication. He stayed in counseling and worked hard on opening up emotionally. About a year later he met a lovely woman, whom he eventually married and with whom he is still quite happily married. I have not heard from Julie.

CHAPTER
9

On-Track and Off-Track Communication

The third time they came for counseling, Keith was angry and wanted to talk about a major argument from the past week. Mary reluctantly agreed.

The argument had started when Mary bravely experimented with the format for resentments they learned at their last session. I say "bravely" because a big part of their problem was a severe power imbalance. Keith was an aggressive, sometimes overbearing guy with a temper. Mary was the opposite: She was frightened, meek, and tolerant to a fault. She rarely expressed her feelings directly, or in straightforward ways. Their marriage wasn't on the rocks, but the power imbalance created significant problems.

As we talked, we reconstructed the argument from the preceding week. Apparently Mary had asked Keith if she could "give him" a resentment. Keith kept his pledge from our previous session, which was to listen to her feelings, including negative ones.

Using the resentment format, Mary said: "When you looked at our phone bill and told me I was wasting hard-earned money by spending so much on phone calls, I was hurt and angry. I was also hurt by your harsh tone of voice."

If she had left it at this, it would have been a good start. Her feelings could have and should have stood alone. Letting Keith know how she felt about his reactions to the phone bill was important information. (As a couple, they needed to talk more openly about budget and spending issues or they would continue to have problems.) But Mary didn't leave it at that. She started justifying her phone calls:

"Most of the calls were to my mom. It's important for me to support her, especially now, when she's sick. She needs me, no matter what you feel about her and about these calls."

Mary added that she had been single for a long time before she married Keith and never before had to account to anyone for her phone bills.

It was probably Mary's insecurity about daring to express a resentment in the first place that led her to start justifying her calls. But the justification about her mom needing support bothered Keith. He thought it implied that he didn't care about his mother-in-law's welfare.

Keith was also bothered by Mary's comment that she never before had to report to anyone about a phone bill. He answered by saying that things change when you get married: "When you're single, your finances are yours alone. When you get married, the finances are shared."

These were his mild opening remarks. Next he said Mary was unfairly accusing him of being cheap. Then came a string of put-downs about her "complaining too much." His voice got louder and kind of aggressive.

"Well, then," Mary said in anger, "you can see why I've been so scared of you. That's why I try to hide phone bills until I catch you in a good mood. You've got a very serious temper problem."

I doubt that Mary would have been as bold about talking about hiding phone bills had she not been in counseling. Nevertheless, Keith's response was overpowering. He answered with insults and an even more threatening posture and tone of voice. He said he didn't want to hear any more of her feelings because she couldn't be trusted.

In a calmer moment, he added:

"You complain that no one ever monitored your phone bills before. Well, I've never been with someone so sneaky that she would hide phone bills from me."

"I guess," Mary said, "I just shouldn't tell you what I feel. I was right all along. You don't want to hear my feelings."

"Maybe you're right," Keith answered. "I was better off when you kept your mouth shut."

"Well," Mary said, "I'm sorry I hid the phone bills. That was dumb. I'm sorry I started all this trouble."

They hit their stuck point. Their discussion ended with Mary's insincere apology. She didn't feel that she had done anything wrong. She only hid the phone bills because he was so overbearing. But she was willing to take the rap to stop the fight.

As Keith told the story in my office, it was clear that he was still fuming about their argument, especially about Mary hiding phone bills.

Mary had put her toe in the water by expressing a resentment. She was frightened by the results and was ready to beat a rapid retreat.

I interceded in a firm way, reminding them that it takes time and practice to learn new communication methods and that mistakes and problems should be expected. In fact—I had warned them at their last session—there could be a temporary increase in tension, because issues that formerly were buried would be brought to the surface.

ON TRACK AND OFF TRACK

In their argument, Mary and Keith locked horns and reached a stuck point. But before they finally stopped talking, they had diverged terribly from what they were trying to do, which was to communicate successfully and cooperatively.

The time was right to tell them about "on-track" and "off-track" discussions, an important concept for people who want to communicate cooperatively. First I put it in context by reminding them that the goal of a loving, cooperative relationship is to work together to satisfy each other.

In this context, communication is on track when it promotes understanding, affection, and teamwork. It is on track when it helps individuals respectfully clarify and resolve their differences without either person dominating or accepting a subservient position. It is on track when it helps a couple solve problems together.

Communication is off track when people use their words in unnecessarily hurtful, or competitive and selfish, ways. Also, communication is off track when one person accepts a subservient position. Sometimes people get off track because they are genuinely confused about how to deal with conflict and problems in a cooperative way. Sometimes they get off track because they are trying to dominate and get their way. Often the distinction between these two factors is blurred, or both factors contribute to the problem.

I told Mary and Keith that people usually don't pause to consider whether their discussions are on track. They keep talking, assuming that everything is fine. This allows unproductive talks to continue uninterrupted, without corrective efforts. But if couples want to stay on track, I told them, they have to *think about* staying on track and monitor their success.

I told them that by watching closely, couples can develop a sense of what is on track and what is not. They can start by learning to recognize when they are far afoot, and then gradually learn to recognize the earliest signs of trouble. Also, they can review some of their discussions to determine how they tend to get off track.

The model for an on-track discussion goes like this:
- "These are my thoughts. What are yours?"
- "These are my feelings. What are yours?"
- "This is what I want. What do you want?"
- "Let's see where we agree. Let's try to understand our differences. Then let's talk about our differences and reach an agreement."
- "What are your ideas about resolving our differences? These are my ideas. What do you think?"

To stay on track in discussions, both persons in a couple must be aware of what they think and feel. They must be able to communicate their thoughts and feelings in a disciplined, cooperative way. And they must be good listeners who seriously consider what their partners say. Also, they must be able to consider and coordinate both their own point of view and the point of view of their partners.

Staying on track is a substantial challenge. In emotional discussions, one topic often sparks thinking about a variety of other topics. It is difficult to stick with an initial issue, to juggle all the emerging issues, and to make sure that everything is addressed. Even skilled communicators have trouble doing this. The challenge of staying on track is made all the more difficult by people who don't pay attention to the issues raised by their partners; they either are poor listeners or egocentric thinkers. They start thinking about their own issues and lose sight of what their partners have said.

GETTING OFF TRACK

I explained that Mary got the discussion slightly off track from the beginning. She said she wanted to express her resentment about Keith's reaction to the phone bill. But then she confused matters by justifying her phone calls, and by slipping in a subtle, implied criticism of Keith. She was raising several issues at once, all under the banner of expressing a resentment. In that sense, her communication was muddled.

In part she got off track because she was new to the idea of direct, straightforward communication. Also, her statements were a reflection of the power imbalance in the relationship, and her own feelings of weakness. She was frightened and felt a need to justify herself for feeling the way she did. So everything kind of came out at once.

If Mary were more experienced at communication and if she felt more powerful, she probably could have divided her communication into three main topics:

1. She was hurt and resentful about Keith's tone of voice and about the fact that he commented on the amount she spent on telephone calls.

2. She saw a problem they needed to discuss as a couple: how to handle financial matters, such as the cost of phone calls. They appeared to have a substantial difference of opinion about that.

3. She was frightened of Keith and therefore had been hiding phone bills. She needed to take her share of responsibility for the inappropriate behavior of hiding bills. She also needed to explain that she was frightened. Then they could discuss how to make their relationship feel safer.

I told Mary it was an important accomplishment that she got out her feelings, even though the process had been somewhat muddled. Gradually she would get more skilled at communicating. To put her difficulties in context, I told her that communication often gets off track when someone feels a little frightened or intimidated by a partner, as she had been feeling. I gave a couple of other examples of how fear or feeling intimidated leads people off track:

1. Sometimes people know what they think or feel but are afraid to say it directly, because they are afraid of the consequences. They only *hint* at what is bothering them.

2. Sometimes people know what they think or feel but are embarrassed about it and try to conceal it. If they show their thoughts and feelings, it is in a confusing or indirect manner.

Mary was interested in this. She said she is often afraid to say what she feels, or embarrassed about it. She gave a few recent examples. A couple of weeks ago she was hurt and angry when Keith didn't send her a birthday card. But she was concerned about "making a mountain out of a molehill." She held back her feelings. Instead of saying what she felt, she later snapped at Keith about trivial, unrelated stuff for a couple of days.

She said, "I often feel hurt about something but don't say it. I get annoyed when Keith hangs out with his friends at times when we could be together. But I don't tell him how I feel. Instead I kind of pick at him later."

Mary's candor was important. She could see how their discussions got confusing when she didn't directly say what she felt. She realized that she needed to start telling Keith when she was hurt. She needed to be more direct. "But," Mary added, "sometimes when I say what I feel, Keith puts me down. I'm scared of that."

Keith was listening attentively, without getting defensive.

"Mary," I said, "it's important that you say what you feel. And Keith, it's important that you respect her feelings."

Keith admitted that he often overreacted.

WHEN A PARTNER IS OFF TRACK

Even though Mary did a poor job of separating issues about the phone bill and started slightly off track, her discussion with Keith still could have been salvaged. When one person begins to veer off track, a partner always has the option of calmly steering the discussion back on track.

Even if someone does something *very* offensive—such as name-calling—nothing is resolved by retaliating. Then you have two people insulting each other, and neither one working to resolve the problem. A basic principle of on-track discussions is the following:

When one person is off track, there is still hope. When both people are off track, they're going to have a fight.

People need to use super-discipline to rise above the errors of their partners so they can redirect a discussion back on track. It's not easy. It's easier to stay on track in the first place than to get back on track once a partner has veered from the straight and narrow.

When Mary muddled her opening remarks, Keith could have put them back on track with a disciplined response that clarified the various issues. For example, he could have said something like this:

"I see you're angry about what I said about the phone bill. It's true I got grumpy about it. I apologize for that.

"You also said we shouldn't need to justify our phone calls to each other. I agree we shouldn't need to justify each and every one, but I believe we have to discuss our ideas about this and other expenses, and have a conversation about a budget. We need to talk about how we spend our money, including which decisions are ours alone as individuals and which are shared.

"I'm not sure what you meant about me objecting to you calling your mom. I hope you realize I want to support her, too. If you don't know that, we need to talk about it."

Unfortunately, Keith lacked the control and analytical abilities to respond in such a manner. Instead he ignored Mary's feelings about his reaction to the phone bill. By ignoring her concerns, he put the discussion further off track. Then he attacked Mary in a loud and aggressive way, taking the discussion totally off track.

POWER ISSUES

Without realizing it, Keith had used a power play. He changed the subject and intimidated Mary into silence. Her initial concern about the way he had treated her was buried, while the focus switched to his anger.

This is one of the most common ways in which couples get off track: The more powerful person brushes aside the concerns of a partner and steers the discussion exclusively toward his or her own issues.

Keith was overpowering. Mary had been scared of him all along. That's why it was hard for her to express any resentment in the first place. By behaving aggressively, Keith made Mary even more frightened.

Ideally Mary would have told Keith she was frightened by his aggressiveness. She would have steered the discussion back on track. But she was more than ready to return to the familiar submissive position. Nevertheless, Mary had one last whimper. After Keith's attack, she angrily proclaimed that she had been hiding phone bills.

Ideally Keith would have realized that they had a serious problem that needed to be addressed: Mary was scared of him and hiding their phone bills.

But they were too far gone at this point. Keith attacked Mary even more fiercely than before. Then Mary apologized to stop the fight.

I told Mary that she was giving away her power and that this was contrary to cooperation. By apologizing when she didn't mean it, she was ending the discussion without addressing her initial issue. Keith and Mary were colluding in allowing their conflict to be resolved by power, with the more aggressive one winning. This wasn't good for either of them because their relationship suffered.

In the course of our discussion at the counseling session, each saw how the conversation had been led astray, resulting in the eventual unsatisfactory resolution. Mary was struck with how frightened she was of Keith and how she needed both to feel safe and to be brave in order to say what she thinks and feels. She could not continue to give away her power. Part of her fear was related to how Keith behaved. Part was her own inherent fearfulness and tendency to retreat. They would not have a cooperative relationship until she stopped running scared.

Mary was able to express her dilemma:

"It's hard for me to tell you when I'm upset at you or angry about something. When I do, sometimes you attack me. We stop talking about the issue I raised, and I have to deal with your anger. So I get scared. I think that's a big part of why I don't say things. I feel what I say will get lost. I stuff my feelings. And the worst part is that I walk around angry at you a lot. It's not fair to you and not fair to our relationship."

Keith said that sometimes he overreacted because of how Mary said things, as in the case of the phone bill. But he also began to realize for the first time how much he frightened Mary. This was important. He genuinely loved her and was concerned that he was pushing her away. He began to see that he needed to learn to modulate his powerful responses.

At this session, something clicked in Mary. She knew Keith loved her, and she began to realize that he wouldn't deliberately hurt her. She resolved, then and there, to renew her efforts to say what she felt. She would not run scared anymore.

When she finally said she was going to stick up for herself, Keith misunderstood. He said, "I'm not going to start kissing your butt."

This is a common misperception. Keith was concerned that if Mary became more assertive he would be pressured to become subservient. That's because people have difficulty understanding the idea of sharing power. They think that either one person must be in control or the other.

I explained to Keith that he needed to give up some of his power to improve their relationship. However, the idea is that they would share power. He would not always get what he wanted, nor would Mary. But usually both of them would be satisfied. Things would change. He would no longer be in control. However, he would have a happy wife who was appreciative, instead of always being angry at him. As a team, they could keep each other happy.

Both Keith and Mary knew that they eventually needed to talk about phone calls, budget, and expenses. But they began to realize that the underlying issue was control, and how they would share the decision-making power.

POWER PLAYS

Mary and Keith were interested in the issue of power and power plays. I explained that sometimes people use power plays because it's the only way they know to settle conflict. They have never seen conflict settled through loving discussion and negotiation.

Sometimes, however, people know there are alternatives but choose to use power plays to try to get their way. They *selfishly* fight for themselves as they attempt to dominate or control their partners. Often they justify themselves because they feel "wronged" about something and believe that they're trying to "right" a wrong. This is their excuse. But it is dangerous thinking. It promotes a type of arrogance:

"I know I'm right and I'll use any means necessary to get my way."

This rationale leads to some of the worst types of marital cruelty. With this mentality, people give themselves permission to abuse power.

Although at times some people choose to abuse power, more often most people use power plays unconsciously, the way Keith had. They get off track from cooperation without realizing it. If Keith were asked whether he deliberately tried to overpower Mary, he would have said no. He thought he was simply being assertive. Like so many people, Keith had been conditioned to use power in controlling ways without realizing this.

Regardless of the motivation or awareness of the motivation, couples who want cooperative relationships strive to avoid abuses of power. It would be unrealistic to imagine ending all power struggles in a marriage: We're so accustomed to relating through power, and so unaware of the various subtle manifestations of power abuse. The commitment that couples can make, however, is to reduce abuses. By being critical and self-critical they can learn to recognize and eventually overcome persistent old habits that interfere with cooperation.

Mary, Keith, and I talked at length over the course of several weeks about how to identify power plays. Neither of them used the most openly aggressive and obvious power plays, such as being violent or threatening violence, or making other threatening gestures, such as pounding fists or pounding walls.

Both of them, but especially Keith, admitted to acting out their feelings or expressing them in a hurtful manner. Mary said that sometimes Keith's body language was frightening.

Both of them used the more subtle forms of power plays. Mary said she was sometimes sarcastic and sometimes rolled her eyes. She also said she sometimes got her way by manipulating Keith with guilt. Keith said he used dirty looks and often sulked either angrily or quietly for long periods until he got what he wanted.

In everyday conversation, Keith was the bigger violator. He often interrupted Mary. Often he would talk in long-winded paragraphs, not giving Mary a chance to respond. He usually tried to "outtalk" Mary. Sometimes he raised his voice. Both of them sometimes called the other one names, but Keith was more vicious about it.

I was impressed that both of them openly admitted so much. Keith had never before realized the extent of his own use of power. He thought of himself as "a nice person and a fair guy."

He was surprised at how controlling he had been, and concerned that Mary was so frightened of him. He could see that he would eventually lose her love if this continued.

CHANGING THE TOPIC

Determined to make good on her commitment to say what she felt, Mary found herself facing a familiar obstacle. In the following session she said she had told Keith what she felt, but he wouldn't listen. She told him she was hurt that he didn't ask about her job anymore, the way he used to in the early years of their marriage.

"Well," Keith answered, "you don't want to make love as much as you used to in the old days."

He changed the topic of discussion. Soon they were talking about their sex life.

"What am I supposed to do?" she asked me. "He changes the subject. I've been trying to tell him what I feel, but he won't listen."

I told Keith that changing the subject was a power play, because he ignored Mary's concern. Then we talked about power plays in which one person—usually the more powerful one—steers the discussion off track to issues that concern him or her.

Using a hypothetical example, I illustrated the most obvious ways in which people get off track: misinterpretation, defensiveness, blaming the other person, discounting, and counterattack.

In my example, one person started the discussion with this statement:

"I'm annoyed that you didn't walk the dogs. You said you would."

Then came responses that illustrated typical ways in which partners change the subject and steer the discussion off track.

By misinterpretation:

"You're telling me that I never do the things I say I'll do. That's not true."

By being defensive:

"Well, you never told me that it was important to walk the dog."

By blaming a partner:

"If you would have been nice to me, then I would have walked the dog."

By discounting or trivializing a partner's concerns:

"You're silly to care so much about walking the dog. There are more important things."

By counterattacking:

"Well, I'm annoyed that you didn't do the shopping you said you would do."

Keith realized that he had used a counterattack when he complained to Mary about their sex life.

SECOND-LEVEL ASSERTIVENESS

As the discussion continued, I told Mary that she needed to learn assertiveness skills. Mary countered by saying that she *was* being assertive: She had told Keith what she felt; the problem was that he wasn't listening.

I agreed that she had made an assertive beginning by telling Keith she was hurt that he didn't ask about her job anymore. However, I said, assertiveness means sticking with it, even when a partner veers off track. I told her I call it second-level assertiveness when you stick with your point even though your partner tries to change the subject.

When Keith switched the topic with a counterattack about a diminished sex life, she could have said something like this:

"If you would like to discuss our sex life, that would be fine. Why don't we deal with my hurt feelings first? I'm hurt you don't ask me about my job. Then we can talk about sex. Or if you believe the two are related, please explain the connection."

"But," Mary said, "he would probably call me a complainer."

So I suggested an assertive response she could make to that:

"If you have a complaint about my complaining, we can talk about that later, too. First I would like you to address the fact that I am hurt that you don't ask about my job anymore."

Keith admitted that Mary had described their interaction well. He could see that he needed to be more receptive to Mary's concerns and slower to push his own agenda.

RECOGNIZING POWER PLAYS

A few weeks after we began discussing power issues, Mary reported with pride that she had been direct with Keith and able to keep a discussion on track. The previous Sunday, when Keith had been grumpy, she defended herself for much of the day and finally spoke up.

"Why are you being so harsh toward me?" she asked. "Did I do something that bothered you?"

"No," Keith answered, "nothing's wrong."

Remembering our talk about power plays and the need for direct communication, Mary told Keith that she felt bad about the way he was acting toward her.

"I know something is wrong," she insisted. "I can see it and feel it. What's eating you?"

Mary's persistence forced Keith to think. He realized what was bothering him. He had spoken with his parents in the morning. Ever since then he was in a bad mood, and taking it out on Mary. He hadn't realized what was happening until Mary persisted in asking. Later he also realized that he often gets grumpy when something is bothering him.

In this case Keith had been off track in his communication because he didn't know what he was feeling. The ultimate way to prevent this problem was for him to become more aware of his feelings. This was a tall order. Yet, how could he expect to have a good relationship with mutual respect for feelings if he didn't know what he was feeling or how his feelings were influencing his behavior?

Keith would have to develop more self-awareness of his feelings if he wanted to avoid this sort of problem.

To stay on track in their communication, people must identify the typical ways in which they get off track. Once the patterns are clear, sometimes all they need is willpower to stay on track. However, sometimes people have to work hard on some of their own underlying problems. This was the challenge for Keith. Many people, like him, have been poorly prepared for loving relationships. For them, the challenge of staying on track is enormous.

As the counseling session continued, Keith committed to gaining more awareness of his feelings and to making a special effort not to take out his frustrations on other family members.

He was especially pleased with this insight and agreement. All along, whenever he had been grumpy with Mary, he would know he was doing something wrong. He hated himself:

"I always felt like a jerk when I was mean to Mary or the kids. I've never before realized what was happening. This discussion will really help me be a better person."

The session was a significant breakthrough. Keith was a loving man with good intentions. He was beginning to see some hard truths. First he had realized that his wife often was scared and intimidated by him. Now he began to understand the ways in which he unfairly hurt her. Keith wanted to improve his marriage. He was inspired. Mary was already inspired. Both of them were highly motivated to make changes. Keith demonstrated his commitment to change by beginning to keep a journal in which he recorded his feelings. This was a way for him to know his own feelings better, which would help promote mutual understanding and communication.

STAYING ON TRACK

In the weeks that followed, Mary and Keith got better at staying on track. In the course of our sessions, we talked about the principles that seemed most important for staying on track:

1. *Self-awareness.* You need to know what you think and feel if you want to communicate with a partner.

2. *Self discipline.* This means speaking carefully, in a non-threatening way; speaking as simply and clearly as possible; and solving one problem at a time without spilling into other problems.

3. *Keeping reason and fairness as priorities.* This means not abusing power and not giving away power. The idea is to promote discussion and understanding.

4. *Listening well and staying focused on the issue at hand.* This means taking partners seriously. You don't discount or negate what they think and feel. You respond to the point without changing the subject.

5. *Coordinating and juggling issues.* This means trying to resolve issues one at a time. If issues are related, it means understanding and making important connections between or among them. If several issues are raised, this means eventually addressing them all.

HANDLING FIGHTS

Both Mary and Keith worked hard on their relationship. Conflict was much more open than ever before. More and more they were able to resolve their differences. However, sometimes Keith would slip into his aggressive attitudes and Mary would become submissive. At other times Mary swung in the opposite direction: She would go overboard because she was feeling braver and more determined to make herself heard.

As a result, every once in a while they would have a vehement fight, as bad as the ones they had before they first came for counseling.

I reassured them that this was part of an overall healthy trend, but urged them to work on calming themselves in these major fights. When they started to "lose it," they needed to refocus on the Basic Cooperative Agreement and rise above the turmoil.

When they got way off track and were fighting terribly, or when they were headed toward a major blowup, they didn't know what to think. I offered them a little script to say to themselves or even to say aloud. It's the type of statement that many couples have told me they find helpful. Here is how it goes:

"Let's stop fighting. This bickering is bad for both of us. Let's remember we're a team. No one is deliberately trying to hurt the other. We love each other. We need to huddle up. Let's calm down, stop fighting, and figure this one out together. I'm sure if I calm down, I can figure out my part of the problem and do something about it.

"We are reasonable people. We are understanding people. We're on the same side. Let's regroup. Let's stop this squabbling and get back on track."

I have found that couples appreciate word-for-word scripts such as these. The ideas in these scripts are not yet part of their own vocabulary. Couples have told me that sometimes in the middle of an argument they hear my voice saying these words. Then they are able to repeat them to themselves. Gradually they internalize this way of thinking, which, in the beginning, was quite different from their original frame of reference.

It's not easy converting from competitiveness to cooperation, going from mistrust to trust. But Keith and Mary were making the transition.

GOING TO BED ANGRY AT YOUR PARTNER

Within a few months, Mary and Keith were more in love than they ever had been. However, one persistent problem remained. There were times when Keith was upset and could not calm himself down to have a productive discussion. In the old days he would have exploded in anger. He stopped doing that. But his new mechanism for handling these sorts of difficult situations was to storm off in anger.

"Aren't there times that people just can't talk?" he asked.

Mary said she hated when discussions ended in a fight. She thought couples shouldn't go to bed angry at each other.

In discussing this issue, I took a middle ground. Indeed, many of the most happily married couples make it a point not to go to bed until their differences are settled.

While the idea of staying up late and talking may sound idyllic, I have known couples who talk when they are very tired and therefore don't always do a very good job of it.

My recommendation is that couples attempt to resolve differences on the spot if they can. If, however, one person does not feel that he or she can talk calmly and rationally at the moment, it is important to go apart. There are times when people are too upset, or too busy, or too tired to talk. On these occasions they should not storm away in a huff. Rather, the cooperative approach is to say why they can't talk and to propose another time in the near future to conclude the discussion. This person should make it clear that going apart is not a power play and that the problem is his or her own inability to deal with the issue at the moment. In other words, the person goes apart to get ready to resolve the matter cooperatively in the near future.

A partner should honor a request to go apart. Discussions are not likely to be successful if one person is not ready to talk. Before parting, the couple establishes a time to resume the discussion, and must make sure to follow through at the pre-arranged time.

This way of going apart worked perfectly for Keith and Mary. Keith was able to calm himself when he got some time alone. Mary was comfortable with this because she was assured that he intended to come back with a clearer mind to settle their differences. It eventually got to the point that Keith could lovingly "ask for space," give Mary a kiss, remind himself that everything would be okay, and calmly walk away for a brief period. Once he knew he could get some space, it got easier and easier for him to calm himself quickly.

APOLOGIES

I knew things were going well for this couple when Keith told me what happened after he forgot their anniversary. Mary was hurt. Keith apologized, but Mary was still hurt after the apology.

In the past, Keith would have complained. He told me he would have said something like this: "I already told you I'm sorry. What do you want from me? What do you want to do, rub my nose in it?"

Instead he apologized several times. He told Mary how much he loved her. He massaged her back and made several suggestions about how to celebrate. Mary picked one idea she liked, and that was what they did.

This marked an enormous transformation in Keith. He went from being a person who brushed aside his wife's feelings to being one who not only paid attention to them but also was persistent in making sure that Mary felt good.

On his own, he had recognized an important, often unnoticed, principle about apologies: Sometimes people have to repeat apologies several times. Just because people say they are sorry does not mean that hurt or angry feelings miraculously vanish instantly into thin air.

CHEER UP THE TEAM

We happily talked about the anniversary episode in one of our sessions. Then we talked further about what I call "cheering up the team."

An emotional aftermath often remains after conflict is settled. One person or both may have residual emotions. That's why it is important to stay on track at this point. Usually this means spending a little positive time together so that everyone is assured that the matter has been completely settled. A smile, a touch, a "How are you doing?" or an "I love you" go a long way toward fixing the mood.

Both Keith and Mary began feeling like members of the same team. They successfully learned to share power. They knew that the best way to resolve conflict was to stay on track in discussions. They learned that if one person got off track, the other could steer things back. If both of them "lost it," one person still could take leadership, snap out of it, and get the discussion back on course. Then, when cooler heads prevailed, apologies would follow. The cooperative model was new to both of them. But they successfully made the transition from competition and power struggles to cooperation and power sharing.

CHAPTER
10

Cooperative Negotiation

"She never wants to make love," David said. "It's not a marriage. We're like roommates, not husband and wife. She's frigid."

"It's true," Linda admitted. "I've lost the desire. I used to try to do it . . . to please David, but I don't even try anymore. I just avoid the whole thing. I know it's a problem."

"It's not like we *never* make love," David added. "Once in a long while I can still coax her into it, but she doesn't get very excited. The only times she has orgasms is when she's on top. Otherwise, nothing."

"You see," Linda said, "all he talks about is sex. I'm not so worried about being frigid, although I have to admit I don't know what's wrong. I'm much more worried that we're not close . . . you know, emotionally."

After a pause, Linda continued, "He hardly ever says he loves me. I feel hurt and rejected. He doesn't seem to care about me. So why should I care about his thing: sex?"

Without having said much, this couple revealed a great deal about themselves and their relationship:

• Both of them were hurt. David was hurt that Linda didn't want more sex; Linda was hurt that David wasn't more emotionally intimate.

• Neither David nor Linda recognized that there might be a connection between their respective hurts.

• Neither of them considered the possibility that Linda's lack of sexual desire might stem from their relationship problems rather than her own inadequacy.

• David seemed unhappy with the sexual position (Linda on top) that brought Linda the most pleasure.

• The two of them were involved in a power struggle.

• They were fighting a lose-lose battle: "You won't give me what I want, so I won't give you what you want."

As the discussion unfolded, it was clear how their sexual relationship had declined. They started "hot" for each other. But from the beginning, David took almost all the initiative in sexual matters, including when, and in what positions, they made love.

Although David wanted Linda to enjoy their time in bed, he was self-centered. As Frank Sinatra put it in his song, David's motto could have been "I did it my way." He wasn't interested in discovering or pursuing what would bring Linda the most pleasure. The two of them didn't discuss sexual preferences. Until they were in my office, David never even knew that Linda had substantial complaints about their lovemaking. She felt that David was a little too fast in his motions. He was a little quick in moving from foreplay to intercourse. He was unimaginative about positions. Sometimes he would let his weight fall too heavily on her. Linda was also upset that David never said anything loving or tender when they were having sex.

Another problem had been timing. After arguments, David was "hot to trot." Linda was not. Her sexuality corresponded with her emotional state. When she was upset about something, she didn't want to be close physically. Yet at these times

David would plunge ahead, never respecting Linda's reticence and lack of passion.

Without discussion, Linda and David had long ago settled their differences about sexual desires and physical preferences: David led and Linda followed. This is how many couples settle their conflict: silently, with one person dominating. Because there is no discussion, the unspoken agreements are often inadequate and breed resentment.

At first Linda and David's unspoken agreements about sex didn't seem to pose a problem. David did what he wanted. Linda accepted this as inevitable.

Neither of them realized that one of the surest ways to lose sexual desire is to have sex when you don't feel like it, and to do things in bed that don't feel good. Linda did both, leading to a loss of sexual desire. Eventually her diminished desire and newfound courage to say "no" started to exceed her willingness to go ahead and "just do it." Then she had little interest in making love.

David and Linda's pattern of settling conflict without discussion—with David dominating and Linda submitting—was not limited to the bedroom. It characterized much of their life together. For example:

1. Most of the holidays were spent with David's parents rather than with Linda's. They never talked about this; they just did it.

2. Housework and household tasks were divided without discussion. (Generally David didn't participate. By default, Linda ended up doing most of the work.)

3. They established individual spending practices, but with different standards. They never discussed finances. Linda tended to skimp on herself, buying mainly necessities for the family; David spent more freely, especially on personal items.

THE CONTROL ISSUE

Linda was hurt by much of what took place between the sheets and also by many other aspects of their relationship. She said she was angry about what she called David's "need to control." She felt he wanted to control her life. David denied this, saying he had absolutely no wish to control her. Linda countered by making reference to some of their big decisions.

"You were the one," she said, "who picked the house we bought when we moved to town."

"I only suggested," David answered, "that we should buy the house I knew you liked."

"How did you know what I liked?" she asked. "You never bothered to ask me."

"Well, you liked it, didn't you? And you're happy with it now, aren't you?"

David was exasperated. "It's like I can't please her," he said, turning to me. "She's never content about things. I *always* consider her when it comes to decisions. This control business is ridiculous."

As we talked, a certain pattern of conflict management became clear. When it came to major decisions, David would enthusiastically assert what he thought the two of them should do. Ultimately he picked their house, the furnishings, the destination and itinerary for vacations, and most of their big purchases. He wasn't consciously trying to control her. In fact, he thought about her interests. Nevertheless, he had a tremendous amount of control. He knew what he wanted, put it forth assertively, and didn't bother to inquire about what Linda wanted. Linda was in a reactive role, responding to what David put forth. Much of the time she thought she was silly to be bothered by this, because his choices were usually good ones. He took pretty good care of her.

What neither of them clearly understood until our discussion is that the *process* of decision-making is as important as the *outcome*. People don't want to feel dominated. They want to feel like equals, with equal power. They want to speak for themselves. People don't want their partners to dictate decisions, even if their partners happen to be considerate and generous.

"But often," Linda conceded, rightfully taking some of the responsibility for David's dominance, "I'm not really clear about what I want."

I explained that their problem in negotiation had two parts. Her part was not getting clear about what she wanted. His part was making decisions without getting her input. They colluded in this process: Linda left a vacuum; David filled it. If he kept pushing for what he wanted, she would never get in touch with her feelings.

To correct their imbalance, David needed to back off. He needed to insist that Linda clarify her thoughts and feelings, or Linda needed to back him off. Then she would have an opportunity to evaluate her own thoughts and desires.

During one session, Linda said that she had rationalized David's dominance by saying, "Marriages are compromises; you don't always get what you want." I explained that this was a serious misunderstanding of the concept of compromise. In good compromises, both people put forth their preferences clearly. There are two proposals on the table. Only then can they see if they want the same thing, or not. If there are differences, only then can they find the middle ground.

Linda confused compromise with submission. Her concept of compromise was "all give" and "no take." In a true compromise, both people agree on what constitutes the middle ground, and each person makes concessions. In the end, both can say, "I did not get exactly what I wanted, but I'm satisfied with this compromise. It's fair. It feels right."

I wanted to make sure Linda understood the importance of stating her point of view in the negotiation process. For emphasis, I put it in dramatic terms:

"You should ask for one hundred percent of what you want."

Linda was quick to protest that this sounded selfish. I clarified, saying that you shouldn't *demand* or *insist upon* what you want, only ask for it. I told her that people often "self-bargain" —that is, make concessions before they even start talking. Then they're forced to make further concessions from their initially stated opening position.

Linda immediately knew what I meant and interjected an example from their lives:

Not too long ago, David wanted to buy a motorboat, which she didn't feel they could afford, but didn't say so. Trying to please David, she made a compromise in her own mind and suggested they buy a small, modest boat. David wanted a big cruiser. So they met each other halfway from their *stated* starting points. This meant that they bought a medium-size boat. David thought it was fair. (He wanted a big one. She suggested a small one. They met halfway.) Because Linda had never stated her true starting point, David never knew that she didn't want a boat in the first place. This made it impossible for them to find the true middle point.

"I think I self-bargain a lot," Linda said.

DOES HE CARE ABOUT ME? CAN I TRUST HIM?

Linda's major complaint in our session was about lack of affection in their marriage.

"Most of the time," she said at one meeting, "I feel like David doesn't care about me. He doesn't even say loving things when we make love.

"Last weekend," she continued, "when we were in Phoenix, we got a late start looking for a restaurant. We were driving around town, trying to pick a place. I suggested one. David pulled in, looked at the menu, and said that I wouldn't be happy there; we should keep looking.

"I said, 'No, it'll be fine. I'm starved.'

"But he insisted we keep driving. He's impossible. He just doesn't listen to me. I was hungry and that restaurant would have been fine. We were driving around for fifteen more minutes. He didn't even care that I was hungry. I'm so angry about that sort of stuff. He never really listens to me."

Linda had been submissive for many years before her anger began to show. The anger gave her a certain amount of power. It was only when she was angry that she could finally allow herself to say what she wanted in a strong way. However, with the accumulated anger, she was sometimes overbearing and unreasonable. Linda couldn't find the cooperative middle ground. At times she relied on her anger too often, and missed opportunities for reasoned discussion.

When Linda started talking about her anger in a session, I made the connection between her emotions and their sexual life. I said, "It's hard to be sexually turned on to someone when you're angry at him."

It was ultimately Linda's anger that allowed her to turn down David's sexual advances. It was in the realm of sexual decisions that Linda eventually began to gain significant power in their relationship. She controlled the lovemaking.

But the power Linda gained was at a cost. Physical intimacy almost vanished from their relationship; she was thinking of herself as "frigid."

BASICS OF NEGOTIATION

"Maybe we just want very different things," Linda said at one point early in our sessions. "We're very different people. I respect many things about David, but we have different interests and, I think, different values—for example, about spending money. We even have different libidos."

I suggested it would be premature for them to decide that their problem was incompatibility. I explained that conflict is inevitable in relationships, even between the most cooperative and compatible individuals, with the most shared interests and values. People always have differences. They have different preferences in day-to-day living, such as where to go for dinner or whether they feel like having sex at a particular moment. They have different outlooks toward life, such as how to spend money or raise children. Life would be boring if people were carbon copies or clones of each other. The issue is not whether people have differences—because they always do—but rather how the differences are settled. Conflict between people who love each other should always be handled directly, in a gentle and cooperative way. People need to learn to negotiate cooperatively from a position of love, searching for solutions that will satisfy *each* person.

Cooperative negotiation is an alternative to the conventional connotation of negotiating, which involves people in adversarial positions bargaining with their own self-interests in mind. People with a Basic Cooperative Agreement are not selfishly looking out for themselves. They are seeking solutions that work all around for both people. They are *finding solutions together*.

Unfortunately, most people have never thought about the possibility of cooperative negotiation. Few have witnessed it. It doesn't occur to them that they could lovingly identify differences, talk about them, and cooperatively search for solutions. Instead, most people do what they were raised to do: either take power or give it away. Some people try to suppress differences. However, most of their differences get settled in a de facto manner (e.g., someone has to take out the garbage; without discussion, someone probably will start doing it). Even on occasions when conflict can actually be avoided, it's usually only temporary. Sooner or later, differences of any significance come to the surface.

I have worked with a number of lovely newlyweds who suddenly felt unexplainable hurt and anger toward each other. Their feelings stemmed from conflict—about issues such as the division of housework—which had been settled *without discus-*

sion. To improve their relationships, many of them merely needed to understand that conflict was inevitable and could be settled through cooperative, open negotiation. They needed to understand the importance of talking out their differences, and were able to do it. Other new couples start to talk about their differences, but get frustrated and give up. They reach their stuck point.

Most couples are like David and Linda: good people who lack both a vision of cooperative negotiation and the skills to carry it out.

For Linda and David, and people like them, it would be premature to conclude that they are incompatible. First, they need to know about the option of cooperative negotiation. Then they need an opportunity to apply it. Only then can they determine where they stand with each other. The outcome might be positive: They might discover that they are more compatible than they ever imagined, or even that seemingly insurmountable differences could be resolved.

THE COOPERATIVE VISION

David was self-centered. At first Linda accepted this reality. She thought relationships were sacrifices. Later she resented it. By the time they came for therapy, both of them knew they needed a change. So they listened with interest when I explained the benefits of making a Basic Cooperative Agreement (BCA), which would mean pooling their energy, working together to take care of each other, and making a commitment to find cooperative solutions to conflict.

"What about all our differences?" David asked.

I explained, "The key implication of a BCA is this: You're not successful in a negotiation process unless you and your partner both feel satisfied at the end. Being satisfied doesn't necessarily mean you get exactly what you wanted in the first place.

"If you want to get exactly what you want every time, if you want to stay in charge of everything, then you shouldn't be in a relationship. You should be single. Single people can pretty much do what they want, when they want. Of course, they miss the pleasure and productivity of a team. Also, two people working together as a team can create many more benefits for each other than they could if they acted alone."

I told them that making a BCA means approaching conflict as a team. Instead of each thinking in terms of self-interest, they would redefine conflict in a cooperative manner by asking these questions:

"How can you and I work as a team to find solutions to our differences? How can we figure things out together so that we *both* feel good? What will work for us?"

Then I explained the three basic cooperative ways to settle differences:

"You find a *compromise* that is acceptable all around. You make *trade-offs*—your way this time and my way next time. Or you find *creative solutions*, such that each person is satisfied without substantial concessions."

I warned that sometimes compromise doesn't work; the middle point wouldn't satisfy either person. Trade-offs, I said, work well if there is balance. However, often one person makes all the concessions. To keep things even, couples should keep an eye on their exchanges—not by measuring each one, but simply by making sure that there is an overall trend of fairness.

I urged them to think especially hard about creative solutions. Too often couples prematurely presume that there could be no solution that would fully satisfy both persons. I said, "It's like the guy who wants to eat Italian food and the woman who wants a healthy salad. Instead of arguing to see who wins, one of them remembers a restaurant that has Italian food and also a great salad bar. Both win."

Linda gave an example of a time the two of them had stumbled on a creative solution. David wanted to go to Hawaii for a vacation. Linda liked the idea, but felt the airfare was prohibitive. David found a coupon that reduced their airfare in half, down to a level within Linda's comfort zone. They went on the trip inexpensively—and both got what they wanted. Thus, even while they had been in a competitive mode, they occasionally stumbled on creative solutions. Surely they could find more of them if they would commit to cooperation.

MAKING OFFERS AND COUNTEROFFERS

Linda and David liked the idea of negotiating cooperatively but said they didn't have a clue about how it would work.

"After making a BCA," I explained, you begin to negotiate by each of you saying what you want. Preferences should be stated in the most nonthreatening ways possible. Nothing should be pushed on the other person. The idea is to find something that works for everyone. This process of stating preferences can't be rushed. If one of you isn't clear on where you stand, it's best to allow time for reflection. Before moving to the next stage of negotiation, you must make sure everything is in the open. You should ask each other, 'Did you say everything you needed to say about what you want and how you feel?' "

I said I knew it would be hard for Linda to say what she wanted. She was used to adapting to other people and trying to please them. Nevertheless, she had to learn new habits.

"Once everything is in the open," I continued, "the two of you can see if your preferences are the same. If not, you begin to look for creative solutions to your differences. If you can't find a creative solution, it becomes a matter of making offers and counteroffers. In other words, someone makes a proposal or series of proposals about how to settle the matter. It would be pushy, and certainly uncooperative, simply to restate your own position. The offers should be compromises or trade-offs, presented in the cooperative spirit of give-and-take, as in:

"These are my ideas about how to settle our differences. What do you think?"

You should always ask your partner for proposals: "What are your suggestions? What's your opinion?"

Cooperating couples engage in this give-and-take process of proposing action plans until one is selected. When one is finally chosen, the couple must be sure each understands it. At this point it's a good idea to review the expectations: "This agreement means you will be responsible for . . . and I will . . ." Before committing to the agreement, both people must be satisfied with the outcome and satisfied that the process was fair and reasonable. Sometimes people aren't sure if they are satisfied. They should take time to think about it, or make the agreement only temporary. ("Okay, let's try it for a week to see how it feels. Let's talk about it again next week.")

A good test of the validity of an agreement is to see if both people can smile at each other after it is made. Both people should be able to say that the agreement is satisfactory—and mean it. If not, something probably is wrong with the process or the outcome, and the couple needs to go back to the negotiating table.

I like to tell couples that they should feel closer to each other after they have negotiated than they did before: "If you feel annoyed, something is amiss."

When agreements are eventually finalized, it is a good practice to set a future time to review progress—to evaluate how the agreements are working and to determine if modifications are required.

POWER PLAYS AND RESCUES

Unfortunately, most people, like Linda and David, have been socialized to feel comfortable in either dominant or submissive positions. It's hard for people to cooperate and act as equals. We're wired for competition. This wiring gives rise to two major stumbling blocks to cooperative negotiation: the tendency to use power plays and the tendency to rescue.

With power plays, people try to dominate and push for their own agenda without giving fair consideration to their partners. They are negotiating selfishly, not cooperatively. With rescues, people give away power. In their zest for harmony, they surrender their role as an equal and "save" their partners from the burden of meeting their needs. With power plays and rescues, the outcome of a negotiation is always one-sided and therefore not equal and cooperative.

Before coming for counseling, most of David and Linda's conflict was settled through a combination of power plays and rescues. In the early stages of their marriage, David maintained dominance while Linda rescued extensively. He led and she followed. More recently Linda had grabbed back some of the power.

In changing to a cooperative mode, this couple faced the challenge of confronting their competitive tendencies. Just like everybody else who has been socialized to adjust to our competitive society, they had to work on reducing rescues and power plays from their interactions.

I explained that two of the *ideal* rules for cooperative negotiation are (1) no rescuing and (2) no power plays. I said "ideal" because these behaviors are persistent and often unconscious habits that never completely vanish. The commitment a couple makes is to recognize these tendencies within themselves, to treat them as impediments to cooperation, and to reduce their occurrence.

Both Linda and David recognized that the rules of "no rescues" and "no power plays" were important parts of cooperative negotiation. They also realized how hard it would be to overcome these tendencies within themselves.

INVALID AGREEMENTS

In negotiating cooperatively, it is important to avoid what I call *invalid agreements*. These are agreements that do not *really* feel satisfactory to one person. Often they are made to settle conflict quickly, often by submissive people to get dominant people off their back. Children, and especially teenagers, make such agreements to get parents off their back. (Sure I won't drink alcohol; sure I'll be home by eleven o'clock.) But these agreements are not true commitments. Sometimes people make them without any intention of following through. More often, people make them under duress, believing that they will comply. But their heart isn't in it. They either ignore or quickly forget the agreements, or comply for short periods before casting them aside.

The problem with invalid agreements is that they don't work. They represent an attempt to short-circuit a difficult negotiation process. As Yogi Berra might put it, "Differences aren't settled until they're settled." People have to learn to stick with the negotiation and tolerate their differences while they continue to seek real solutions.

If differences are large, couples have to work hard, sometimes for prolonged periods, until they can legitimately resolve them. Rather than rushing into invalid agreements, it's better to acknowledge differences and extend discussions over several days or more, until a good agreement can be made. No one said negotiation would be easy—or quick.

GRABBING POWER

Both Linda and David were willing to examine their own difficulty in sharing power. David realized that he acted unilaterally and tended to dominate in decision-making. Linda saw that she had been submissive for many years—a pushover. Now she sometimes acted submissively and sometimes erupted in unforgiving anger.

One way David maintained his dominance was by ignoring or ridiculing Linda when she stated her preferences. For example, when Linda finally mustered the courage to say that she wanted to spend time with her parents over the holidays, he dismissed this as "silly" because her family was "so dysfunctional."

Even on occasions when David conceded to Linda's wishes, he sometimes laughed at her, communicating the message "It's silly, but since you want this, I'll do your (dumb) plan." Thus even when Linda prevailed, she still felt bad about the outcome—and about David.

Another way David dominated the relationship was by outtalking Linda. He would intimidate her by reminding her of past mistakes. He would warn her, in a very solemn tone, that if they did as she wanted, she would be "responsible for the outcome." It didn't take much of this sort of talk to discourage Linda.

David also knew how to coax what he wanted from Linda with appeals such as: "Oh, c'mon," or "Oh, please," or "I'll be so disappointed if . . ." This type of power play was particularly successful in the sexual arena during the early years of their marriage.

In our sessions, David began to think about his need to get his way. When Linda asked him why it was so important that she clean the dishes and the kitchen *immediately* after dinner, David paused to think. He realized that this was how things had been done in his home as a child. In his mind, this was the correct way to do things: "If Linda loved me, she would do the dishes right away." Even as he uttered these words, he could see it didn't make sense. David realized that Linda and he were making their own life together. It shouldn't be defined by one person's earlier experiences. It should represent some sort of combination of what the two of them brought to the relationship. David was beginning to see how much he really did try to control things with Linda.

GIVING AWAY POWER

How and why did Linda give away power? The biggest reason was her mistaken concept of a relationship as a compromise (i.e., a sacrifice). In addition, Linda had some other thoughts that led her to give away power:
- The myth that good relationships are free of conflict. "Don't make waves."
- The idea that if one person gives (or "is nice"), the other will inevitably return it all. (This simply is not true in a competitive situation.)
- A fear of losing love: The theory is that you are liked or loved for what you give, and for what you do for the other person. If you stop giving, you might lose your partner's affection.
- A feeling of low self-esteem: "I don't deserve anything; it would be selfish to ask or insist. My opinions and preferences and desires aren't important."
- The idea of putting the other person first: "Take care of your partner. It's your responsibility to please, and your fault if your partner is not satisfied."
- A fear of failure: "I'd be responsible if I got my way and things didn't work out as planned."
- A fear of criticism: "I'd never hear the end of it if I took the lead and made a mistake."
- A sense of resignation: "There's no point in saying what I want. He'll get his way anyway."
- Low expectations for a relationship: "Just accept things. It could be worse. At least he doesn't beat me, have affairs, or abuse alcohol."

Linda realized that sometimes her relationship with David may have appeared to be more nearly equal than it was, as if she were making choices. However, her choices were often speculative guesses at what would please David. The guesses were made in fear—fear of David's disapproval or discontent if he didn't get what he wanted.

David didn't realize that Linda felt intimidated. He saw her making what appeared to be free choices, and thought she was happy. He was surprised about how dissatisfied she had become.

In our sessions, David sometimes tried to blame Linda for her own dissatisfaction. He kept saying, "You never told me. How could I know you were this unhappy? I thought you were doing what you wanted to do."

I validated David's sense of surprise about Linda's unhappiness. I also explained that the only protection against such surprises is to know your partner well. You need to watch her closely to make sure she is saying what she feels and what she wants. If not, you need to ask questions.

Linda said, "You could have asked me how I was doing. You could have been asking me what I wanted."

"But," I said to Linda, "you must admit that you mystified things by your attempts to appease and avoid trouble."

Linda agreed. For many years she had put up with David's dominance. She kept thinking things would change for the better; she told herself that David loved her, and made excuses for his self-centered ways. When her anger finally erupted—after being repressed for so long—there was a huge backlog of resentment. Linda often repeated, "How could someone who claims to love me so much have treated me so poorly?"

A great deal of damage had been done by Linda and David's inability to share power.

EMOTIONAL INTIMACY

It was a classic case of locked horns, with the man wanting more sex and the woman more emotional intimacy. Linda was not satisfied with the emotional part of the relationship and therefore didn't feel sexual. David wanted more sex but had been unable to respond to Linda's emotional needs.

One of Linda's complaints was that she hated that David liked to eat dinner in front of the television. She wanted his attention. She wanted closeness. But David insisted that television was a good way for him to decompress after a tough day in the office. Linda kept asking for more attention and time together. To have more shared time, Linda had bent to his desires and did the sorts of things he liked to do. But he didn't reciprocate. They rarely dressed up and went to the theater or art galleries, or to nice restaurants, which were the type of activities she enjoyed. David basically did what he wanted, and almost never negotiated a settlement about sharing time. His self-centeredness was an important part of their problem.

Linda's lack of assertiveness was the most obvious way that she contributed to their power imbalance. As we talked in our sessions, we found a more subtle problem. Linda was committing one of the classic errors of negotiation: making concessions without letting her partner know. For example, she generally liked to stay up late. But she would go to bed by 10:00 P.M. so they could get up at the crack of dawn for early-morning walks — something David liked. David never knew this was a concession, and thought Linda wanted to walk as much as he did.

In a lighter moment, when Linda complained about the suspense thriller videos they often rented, David said, "I thought you liked them."

"You gotta be kidding," Linda answered. "Now that we're bringing concessions into the open, you better realize that renting suspense thrillers was about as big a concession as they come. I hate those movies. I think they're horrendous."

After many years of tolerance, Linda finally became fed up that David didn't seem to want to do the things she liked and didn't want to spend more time together. She had started to say what was bothering her, often in a terribly harsh and judgmental way. She would say:

"You're cold and heartless. You don't care about me. You want to control me."

With remarks such as these, Linda hoped to start a discussion. But David tended to avoid personal discussions, especially when he felt he would be criticized. By avoiding discussions, once again David got his way.

During one of our early counseling sessions, David defensively answered one of Linda's complaints about the lack of emotional closeness by saying:

"You know, I gave you a little, and you see, you want a lot."

Linda replied, "I don't ask for that much."

This was a revealing exchange. I suggested a different perspective, that people *should* ask for, and share, a lot of closeness in a loving relationship.

"Don't you two want this?" I said. "Linda, you've been asking for closeness, I assume you want a large amount of it."

Linda backtracked and admitted she did, but added that she would settle for even a little at this point.

"What about you?" I asked David.

He thought for a while. He said he wanted more closeness, too, but admitted that this was not his strong suit. He said he wanted to work at it. However, he hated when Linda called him cold and uncaring. He felt that her criticism and disapproval were pushing him away. He was fending her off emotionally.

They had locked horns on the issue of emotional intimacy. The more Linda criticized David, the more he backed away. The more David backed away, the more she criticized.

In one of our sessions, we recognized that they had a parallel problem: David was fending Linda off emotionally. Linda was fending David off sexually.

On a positive note, I reminded them that both wanted to improve the relationship. Linda had said she would like more sexual intimacy if the relationship improved. David now acknowledged that he would like more emotional intimacy, but felt that Linda's anger and harsh criticism made it hard to overcome his own hang-ups about being close.

TAKING TURNS

David and Linda's present issue concerned their sex life. I made it clear to them that sexuality, although an important focus of attention, was not the heart of the problem. It was clear to me that sharing power was the central issue, and their inability to cooperate and share power had adversely affected their sex life. Nevertheless, sex was very much on their mind. The topic had to be addressed. It also seemed important to talk about sex and sexuality to help Linda regain her self-esteem, because she thought of herself as frigid.

In one of their early counseling sessions I told them that I don't think of a woman's disinterest in sex in terms of "frigidity." The term gives a distorted meaning to the problem. Rather, I said, I think in terms of people becoming turned off to sex, or at least to sex with a particular partner.

As the two of them discussed the details of their sex life, it became clear to them what had been turning off Linda. David had started with all the control over sex. He did all the initiating. Linda was making love when she didn't feel like it. She was unhappy about what they did in bed. She wasn't asking for what she wanted. Furthermore, and perhaps more important, Linda was feeling hurt and distant from David.

Eventually the tables turned: Linda began resisting David's advances. More and more she found herself in the position of fending him off. She was on guard, pushing him away. From this defensive position, she had lost touch with her own sexual urges. Meanwhile, David was hurt by the many rejections.

The good news, I reassured them, was that if they wanted to regain their initial sexual excitement, there was a great likelihood it could be done. For this to happen, however, their relationship had to improve so that Linda would feel more warmly toward David. Meanwhile, David had to stop pressuring Linda to have sex. If he stopped pressuring, and their relationship improved, Linda's own sexual urges would eventually return.

I said it was essential that they deal with emotional intimacy at the same time as sexual intimacy. We talked about how they had separated the two: Sex was his issue; emotional closeness was hers. If they wanted to be happy, they had to work on both. This seemed to be the only way, and the fair way, to settle their differences.

I told them about a method that would probably improve their sexual relationship. The way it works is simple: A couple takes turns initiating sex. If he goes first, he would ask Linda to make love when he felt like it. She could accept or refuse his proposal. Then it would be her turn to initiate lovemaking. At this point David could *not* initiate sex again until after Linda had taken the initiative. They would keep taking turns. If they stuck to the program, David would be spared all the rejections. Linda would have significant control over the frequency of making love and would not have to be resisting a barrage of pressure. She could get out of the defensive position of pushing David away, and eventually realize that her own sexual fulfillment depended on opening up and taking the initiative.

I told them that this process requires time and enormous patience, especially on David's part. It might be quite a while before Linda started seeking sex. But in reality, I told David, he had no choice except to be patient. If he rushed, he would be pressuring Linda. That obviously was what already had led her to resist his advances.

I warned Linda that the process would be somewhat confusing to her. She might feel internal pressure, a sense of obligation about having sex. She might blame this on David, and resist more. Or she might give in to it, and feel bad about having sex before she felt ready. On the other hand, her part of the deal was to watch for her sexual urges and to go with them. In that way they could regain their physical intimacy.

Although this method sounded mechanical to them, they could see its merit. It allowed Linda to regain her sexual desires, and it protected David from repeated rejections. It was even-handed. It was a form of cooperation, with each breaking old patterns of interaction. By taking turns they could learn to share responsibility for sex.

Several weeks after they agreed to take turns, I gave them exercises to do at home that were physical but nonsexual. The exercises involved touching and pleasuring each other. They would exchange back rubs, foot massages, and other types of physical touch. To succeed in these exercises, they needed to communicate their desires and preferences. But they could not go from the exercises to intercourse. That was a rule. The idea was for them to have a safe situation in which to explore desires and preferences, and to work on issues related to giving, receiving, and asking for physical touch. They needed more openness of expression in their physical relationship. They needed to talk to discover how to satisfy each other.

As our dialogue continued in the sessions, we worked through David's insecurities about Linda being on top. We also talked of sex as a metaphor for their relationship: Sex is not good unless both people get what they want; it has to be wonderful for both of them.

EMOTIONAL NEGOTIATION

Sometimes people negotiate about specific, clear-cut behaviors—for example, where they go on vacation or how they divide housework. On other occasions people negotiate about psychological or emotional issues. At this point in their counseling, Linda and David needed to negotiate about emotional issues.

Linda agreed to stop being so harshly critical of David. She was right to recognize that David had problems in emotional intimacy. But calling him names and putting him down weren't helping. If she wanted the relationship to improve, she had to accept David's starting point. Then she could constructively ask for the changes she wanted.

David agreed to strive for more closeness in their relationship but said that he needed help with this. Specifically he wanted to know what Linda wanted.

Linda spelled out her needs. One thing she stressed was a desire for greater equality when they negotiated differences. She also wanted more time together, more shared activities, and David's willingness to do more things she liked to do. David agreed to it all.

"Please," Linda asked, "don't do this just to please me. Only do it if it sounds like the kind of relationship and kind of closeness you want."

David admitted it was a new idea to him but said he wanted to try it.

In the beginning they had a few problems with the new arrangement. David would go places with Linda and do some of the things she liked to do. But he made it sound as though it was a big favor.

Linda kept saying, "Don't do it unless you want to do it."

David began to realize that you don't make a partner feel good by begrudgingly spending time together. He stopped complaining, and even started to enjoy some of the shared activities. Soon he noticed that Linda wasn't criticizing him as much, and that she seemed more appreciative of him.

COMING THROUGH EMOTIONALLY

Over the next few weeks we talked a great deal about emotional intimacy. Linda mentioned an event that had occurred a few days before one of our meetings. She had called David on the phone to tell him about an exceptionally bad day at work: In the morning her boss had embarrassed her in front of a group of peers. In the afternoon her car broke down, causing her to miss several meetings. Later her boss picked on her a second time.

After work, Linda again told David about her awful day, hoping for support.

David's answer was, "I'm sorry." Then he paused. "I'm tired, too. I had a tough day." Then he withdrew.

Linda was angry. Later she told David that she didn't feel he was "there" for her.

"But I was tired, too," David answered.

This was when we talked about people "coming through" for each other. Sure, David had been tired, but just average tired. However, Linda had had exceptional needs that day. David missed the cue. On days such as these, we all agreed, partners have to rise above their own fatigue and meet the challenge. They need to come through for the people they love. This is how intimacy works.

We talked more about a caring consciousness. We talked about people making their partners feel special by a variety of methods such as writing little love notes, picking up small presents, getting up at the crack of dawn to say goodbye when one person has to leave early for a trip, rubbing the tense neck and shoulders of a partner, and putting a blanket over a partner when he or she falls asleep in the living room.

As a child, David never experienced this sort of caring. It was new to him. But he was beginning to understand what it means to be really close, loving, and caring. He wanted a better relationship.

TRUSTING EACH OTHER

The taking-turns strategy in bed provided some of the usual twists and turns. By their agreement, Linda was to go first in terms of initiating sex. David was pretty good the first week. He stopped his verbal come-ons. However, he did attempt to transform some physical touches into something sexual. Linda dodged his efforts and complained about them at our next session. The following week, all was quiet. No sex. No propositions. But David complained about Linda's lack of physical intimacy. I advised him that such complaints are another form of pressure. I told him he needed to back off so that Linda could feel her own feelings, in her own due time; the more he pressured, the more she would be in a "leave me alone" posture, not a posture likely to lead to sexy feelings. Anyway, I predicted, there would have to be a breakthrough in emotional intimacy before the sexual intimacy would follow.

The next week, again no sex, but again some physical and even one verbal advance from David.

This led to a "See, he won't change" and a "See, she won't change" discussion.

"He won't back off," Linda said. "He wants to control me."

"She always says I want to control her," he answers. "I've backed way off. I just want some physical intimacy. I feel so rejected."

"And how do you think I feel?" Linda asked. "You won't respect me."

"Well," David said, "we each agreed we wanted to make the other one happy. I've been trying to be more emotionally giving. You're supposed to be more physically giving."

"I want that, but it's impossible when you won't back off."

David explained that it's hard not to get sexual gratification. He feels hurt and wounded.

But that was the point. He needed what he wanted on his own timing. He felt it had to go his way. He was finding it hard to give up control and to allow Linda the space to regain her own sense of initiative. We talked about this at length, relating it to their decision-making process in which David was almost always in the lead. I suggested that he was going to have to be much more patient. He had to give up control.

I also started talking about the issue of trust. David had to trust that if he didn't force the issue, Linda would rise to the occasion. He had to find out what his relationship would be like if he stopped trying to control it.

I told Linda that I knew she faced a dilemma. She wanted to move forward by initiating physical intimacy, but it was hard to advance because she didn't want to feel pushed.

As the discussions evolved over the weeks, Linda admitted that part of her reluctance to get physical was because she saw it as losing power. "It would be giving him what he wants. The one thing I control in our relationship right now is sex."

Again it was the issue of trust. Linda had to believe that if she let down her guard and stopped being angry, David would work on changing his behavior.

She also had to realize that it wasn't just that David was a "bad guy," selfishly doing sex his own way. She had been an equal partner in creating the problem. She had given away her power. She was never clear about her sexual preferences. She was never assertive about turning down sex when she didn't feel like it. She had to stop putting all the blame on David.

Neither Linda nor David trusted that the other would change. Both were finding it difficult to give up control. Both were blaming the other and finding it hard to focus on his or her own part of the problem.

I pointed out that their relationship could not improve unless they broke through on the trust issue. If they didn't believe their partner would change, then they would remain entrenched in their own behavior. "You have to agree to change at the same time, and you have to trust each other. You have to do your part of things *right* and believe that your partner will change, too. If you don't, nothing will change. If you want to continue to mistrust each other, there's no point in pursuing counseling."

We found that one way in which they could increase their trust of each other was to talk more openly about personal issues, both about their past and their day-to-day lives. They started to take a little time each day just for talking. They were willing to open up and be vulnerable in this way. Although the discussions helped with trust, a certain standoffish quality persisted in their interactions.

YOU GO FIRST

Shortly after our discussion about trust, an incident occurred that shed some light on the problem. David had been conscientiously trying to "be there" for Linda. One day, however, he backslid and blew up at her over some little matter. He apologized profusely for the incident. It really looked as if he wanted to take care of her feelings. He wanted to do something about the unnecessary hurt he had caused. He took such good care of her that he was late to work that day. This was a real change—making the relationship a priority over work. David felt good about how he handled his apology.

That evening he came home from work late, hoping his apology had "worked" and that Linda would approach him warmly. Meanwhile, Linda was in the living room, lying on the couch. She hoped he meant what he had said in his apology and that he would approach her warmly.

He was disappointed that she didn't greet him at the door. She was disappointed that he didn't come over to the couch to greet her. They watched each other like nervous cats. They were playing the mistrustful game of "you go first," passively and competitively putting the burden on the other person to make the first move. Neither person was striving to be a "love leader," to lead the way to cooperation. The tension finally erupted into an argument over some trivial matter. When we discussed this incident, they recognized that both had to break through on the trust issue.

HELPING EACH OTHER ALONG

On many occasions I have told couples that they can make very substantial commitments about how to be with each other—including major commitments to change—and successfully keep to their word. I have gone so far as to warn some couples on the brink of divorce that they must stop slinging insults—starting today, and forever—if they want to save their marriage. It can be done. People are capable of extraordinary accomplishments if they set their minds and hearts to it.

With agreements, however, mistakes and setbacks should be expected. It's hard to change old patterns of behavior. For example, when Linda agreed to be assertive and to say what she felt, it would have been naive to expect that she would immediately and always be able to do this. Similarly, it would be expecting too much to think that David would never again exclude Linda from the decision-making process, even though he had committed to including her. The commitments they made were not to immediate, total success. Rather, they were to strive toward the goal. It also would have been naive to think that David could have immediately, completely backed off from asking for sex, or that Linda would suddenly feel tremendous sexual passion.

Change is gradual. Couples need to support each other in making changes. In this process, broken agreements are to be expected. Sometimes it is simply human error. Sometimes it means the agreements were not good ones. Perhaps too much was expected too soon.

Linda and David tended to take the other person's broken agreements as confirmation that change would never occur. I suggested that they approach broken agreements differently, with an assumption of goodwill. In cooperative relationships, mistrust over broken agreements is replaced with gentle suggestions and calm discussions to help a partner succeed. This requires super discipline. We talked about super discipline in the context of David's sexual advances.

I recommended that Linda begin with gentle reminders to help David keep the agreement. For example:

"David, you're asking me to make love. Remember please, it's my turn to ask. You're supposed to wait. Let's stick with our plan."

I told Linda she could cooperatively express her feelings. For example, she could say:

"David, I feel annoyed that you're asking me to make love, because we had agreed to take turns."

If the problem recurred, the next step would be to start a calm discussion:

"David, you agreed we would take turns and that you would give me some space. What's happening? Why do you keep suggesting we make love?"

If the first discussion failed, she could suggest a more serious second discussion: "We already talked about this problem last week. I thought we got to the bottom of it, but apparently we didn't. We need to get to the bottom of our problem. What's wrong? Why won't you back off and give me a chance to take the initiative?"

In most cases, couples who want to cooperate can work things out with gentle reminders and calm discussions. If it goes beyond this point, strong feelings become part of the discussion: "I'm frustrated and annoyed that we've already had two discussions about this problem. Let's get it solved. I'm not going to feel good about keeping to my agreements if you don't do better about keeping to yours."

If one person continually fails to keep agreements, the other person will eventually issue an ultimatum: "Keep your agreements or I'm going to withdraw my cooperation."

Over time, Linda learned how calmly to ask David to stop pushing for sex when it was her turn to initiate. David learned to remind Linda when she was calling him names such as "heartless" and "uncaring." They both worked as a team, helping each other make changes.

HOT AGAIN

Linda and David's relationship improved slowly over time. Certain events were critical to the change. David was shocked when he began to discover how very controlling he had been in the relationship. It really hit home when we talked about how hard it was for him to give up control of sex and to allow some space for Linda to take the initiative.

Linda began to see some of her problems. She realized that she didn't know how to be strong and assertive without staying angry and sometimes resorting to name-calling. She could see that this was pushing David away. She also could see how she surrendered power when she wasn't angry.

Linda worked on assertiveness. David worked on sharing power.

A significant breakthrough occurred one day, after work, when the two of them were about to leave for the mall. David was tired and told Linda to drive. She, too, was tired, but started to walk to the driver's seat.

"Wait, I'm sorry," David said. "I did it again, didn't I? I don't want to be telling you what to do. Do you want to drive, or do you want me to drive?"

"I'd like to drive," Linda said, "but thanks for asking."

Although a minor incident, Linda could see that David wanted to share power. He was beginning to back off.

At about the same time, after approximately two months of occasional pressure, David finally stopped pushing for sex. In one of our sessions, he said:

"I'm tired of pushing. It's wrong to push. If you don't want it, I don't want it either."

Linda was delighted.

Little changes began to make a big difference. As David started to share power, he was also showing more clearly that he cared. Linda noticed that he would ask her how she was feeling about the temperature before adjusting the thermostat at home. He was showing more consideration.

When David backed off from pushing for sex, Linda dabbled with initiating it. Their lovemaking was a little tense at first, in part because something was different: They were talking. Linda was asking for what she wanted in bed.

It took several months without pressure before Linda felt safe in bed. As her trust increased, she got bolder in the sexual arena. Although self-conscious about it, David started whispering loving words to Linda while making love. This was new. Linda responded with passion, which reinforced David's interest in saying these nice things. They felt closer. As the relationship improved, Linda felt more and more sexy. Going from a cold relationship to a warm one had thawed her out. The whole idea of "frigidity" now seemed absurd to them. David was pleased with the passion he felt from Linda and began to think of himself as—and joked about being—a great lover.

David and Linda were doing better about bringing their differences into the open and negotiating. Linda was much more assertive. She raised some issues that had bothered her for a long time, such as the one about where they spend the holidays. They agreed to go to her parents' home for some of them. They also had the idea of having all the parents come to visit on Thanksgiving.

David and Linda negotiated other tough issues as well, such as the division of housework and the budgeting of financial resources. Although the discussions were sometimes heated and tense, they managed to get everything into the open and to settle these important matters.

There were setbacks along the way. At one point David realized that he was trying so hard to accommodate Linda that he was conceding on matters that were important to him. To keep the harmony, he had swung too far in the opposite direction. Ironically, Linda made a similar mistake. Because things were feeling better and her anger had dissipated, she relapsed a little about being totally honest about what she wanted. She was uncomfortable with conflict, too eager to settle matters quickly, and afraid of being selfish and too demanding. As a result of their excessive "niceness," both Linda and David made a few invalid agreements. However, they had fully embraced the spirit of cooperation and were able to recover.

Nine months after we began talking, David and Linda were a happy, sexy, and emotionally close couple. Each had grown tremendously.

CHAPTER
11

Unconscious Barriers to Intimacy and Communication

Cathy made an appointment to see me after reading my newspaper column about steps to take before deciding on a divorce. Over the telephone she said she had a serious problem with her husband, Jerry, whom she described as cold, cruel, and domineering. She said she was terribly depressed and wasn't sure what to do about her marriage.

When I met Cathy, I found her to be delightful and energetic. She was not clinically depressed, but was miserably unhappy and filled with anger toward her husband.

At her first session she talked with much enthusiasm, obviously relieved to discuss problems that had been bothering her for a long time. Mainly she discussed her unhappy childhood and unhappy marriage.

As a child, her parents had been demanding, disapproving, and harshly critical. Although they now lived far from her home in Tucson, Arizona, it was apparent that Cathy was profoundly tied to them: She was still seeking the support of her mother and the approval of her father, goals that neither she nor her two brothers had ever been able to attain. Her dad was not one to give praise. He called himself a "great motivator" but could more accurately be described as hypercritical. Nothing was ever good enough for him. Throughout her childhood, Cathy felt inadequate and inferior. She also felt that her father didn't love her. Cathy's mother generally ignored her father's critical treatment of the children, and escaped family tension through volunteering for community service. Cathy thought that her mother probably felt supportive of her but was too intimidated to provide protection.

Growing up in this cold and hostile environment, Cathy suffered from low self-esteem. Despite her school success, she felt bad about herself. During her teen years she gained acceptance by peers mainly by drinking and taking drugs. She also used her physical attractiveness as a lure to men.

At age twenty-one she met Jerry, the man who was to become her husband. At that time she was thoroughly confused about her own identity and direction in life. She didn't know whether to continue in college or get a job. She felt bad about herself and her relationships with men. She had little confidence about her future. Jerry offered an alternative: marriage. He would support the family. Cathy was relieved to find someone who could take control over her life, a task that had come to feel unmanageable.

Cathy liked Jerry, and was pleased that he seemed sincere in his intentions. He was different from so many other men, who only wanted to use her sexually. But she didn't feel entirely comfortable with him, and eventually entered the marriage with apprehension. In the next nine years they had two children, first a girl, then a boy. Cathy devoted herself to the children while Jerry successfully advanced in his career.

Even before the honeymoon ended, Cathy began to see that Jerry was demanding and controlling. He wanted things done his way and on his timing. When he was upset about something, he would become hostile and aggressive.

As the relationship evolved, Jerry was the one who determined the division of labor. He also had his way when he wanted sex. "Everything goes his way," Cathy said. "He even has to have the best cut of meat when we eat together. He insists on it."

Jerry's domination extended to their recreational life. Cathy was outgoing and wanted to have fun. Jerry vetoed most of the entertainment activities she suggested. He also didn't enjoy outdoor activities. He didn't even want to eat at restaurants. His idea of fun was to stay home and do his hobbies. The only other shared activity was going to church on Sunday. Jerry was quite religious.

Lacking in self-confidence, Cathy didn't stick up for herself. Instead she followed the pattern she had learned as a child, of trying to win the approval of a powerful male figure, this time her husband. She worked hard trying to give Jerry everything he wanted. She thought if she could be a "good enough wife and mother" that her love would someday be reciprocated. Over the years, however, she began to feel that she could never please this man, no matter how hard she tried. She became demoralized and unhappy about the marriage. Her resentment grew as she continued to accommodate his demands.

One of the big sore spots was housework. Cathy tried to meet Jerry's expectations for cleanliness. But he always found something wrong, whether it was hair in the sink or smudges on the woodwork. His demands were extreme. In her words, "Everything had to be spotless. Everything had to be put away. He couldn't tolerate even the smallest mess. When a mess was made, it had to be cleaned instantly. And with two kids that's impossible."

Cathy couldn't keep it up, and anyway didn't really aspire to the aseptic standards that Jerry demanded. When she protested about the standards, he criticized her, saying she was not pulling her weight in the marriage. When she protested further, he would withdraw angrily, giving her the cold shoulder, sometimes not even talking to her for several days. His characteristic way of expressing anger, either by attack or withdrawal, left Cathy walking on eggshells, worried about what he would do next. When he attacked or withdrew, she felt unloved.

Cathy said that Jerry also placed unreasonable demands on their children, especially the younger one, who had a physical disability. When the children disappointed him, they were harshly reprimanded. This disturbed Cathy, who defended them whenever she could. But she paid a steep price for this because Jerry would attack her for "grabbing power." Nevertheless, Cathy didn't want to remain neutral about his harsh treatment of the kids, as her mother had been when her father attacked her when she was a child.

Cathy soon realized that Jerry was negative about life and about people in general. He viewed the world as a jungle of untrustworthy individuals filled with exaggerated self-importance. He was suspicious and critical of almost everybody and skilled at identifying flaws.

Early in their marriage, Cathy accepted Jerry's scathing put-downs of other people. But Jerry's negativity went too far and eventually became a major source of tension in the relationship. Cathy began to feel uncomfortable because she valued relationships and wanted friendships. But Jerry would put down everyone, including the people she liked. He demanded all her time for himself and never wanted to socialize with others. Cathy became more and more isolated.

Her isolation—partially the consequences of staying home with children and partially the result of her husband's rejection of friends and acquaintances—was a serious problem for this couple.

Even with all her complaints, Cathy said she still loved Jerry and recognized his admirable qualities. He was intelligent and a good provider. He was successful in his career, and had worked his way up to a top accounting position at the cable television company where he worked. When he wasn't angry or under pressure he could be loving and supportive at times, and even great with the children.

But Cathy was angry about the way Jerry had dominated their marriage and about the way he could be cruel to her. As she talked, it sounded as though she had many valid gripes. Undoubtedly Jerry was a controlling individual.

When Cathy started counseling, she did not understand her own role in the marital problems, except that she had allowed the power imbalance to continue. She was angry at herself: "I shouldn't have let him walk all over me." But she didn't know exactly what she could have done differently. She didn't understand how she had colluded in the problem. Lacking this insight, she angrily blamed Jerry for everything.

Cathy mentioned divorce. She said she would like to be free of this marriage, and would feel relieved except for two problems: (1) She was concerned about the children. (2) She was dependent on Jerry, both financially and emotionally. She did not feel she could hold her own in the world. She lacked self-confidence.

The prospects of staying with Jerry were not appealing. The prospects of life as a single person were also grim. It was scary. Cathy realized that she had not totally rejected the idea of ever fixing it with Jerry. She had some respect for him. She also felt it was important at least to give it a chance because of the children. And she was candid about another fact: She was afraid of going out on her own.

At this point in life, Cathy had no marketable skills. She had never worked, nor had she completed a college education. Although she knew she could find a low-paying job of some sort, the challenge of raising children and supporting the family as a single parent seemed overwhelming. She realized she needed to prepare herself for the job market.

As Cathy spoke, I sympathized with her complaints and resentments about Jerry's dominance. I also reflected on the intensity of her anger. She had waited much too long to get help.

Her desire to leave was evident, but it was equally clear that she felt she had to stay right now. For one thing, she had her children to consider. If she left without trying to work things out, she might unnecessarily harm them. In any event, before she would be capable of leaving, it seemed she would need to feel good about herself and change her own life. I urged her to think about developing her personal self-esteem and self-confidence. She needed to break her isolation. She also had to pull herself out of a position of economic dependence. If she did all that, she would be better able to evaluate her relationship objectively, from a position of strength.

It was also important that she could understand her own collusion in Jerry's dominance. As she spoke, I pointed out that there had been ways in which she had given away power. She had not been assertive about her needs. Jerry claimed a dominant position, but she accepted a submissive one.

THE INTEGRITY POSITION

During her second session, I introduced Cathy to an approach to a troubled relationship that I call the *integrity position*. It is a stance I recommend to people who want to fix, or might want to fix, their relationship, but are not sure their partners will be willing to change, or whether the closeness and love they once felt could ever return.

With the integrity position, a person works on his or her own contribution to the relationship problem. At the same time, the person insists that the problem is "two way" and cannot possibly be resolved without a partner's participation.

This is common sense. I explained the logic to Cathy: Unless you choose to end an unhappy relationship, you need to keep working at it. Because you can't change your partner, you work on yourself. *You* are the only person you can change. At the same time, you don't want to give the message that you alone are responsible for the relationship problems, nor that you could fix things alone. So you continue to ask your partner to get involved, and keep stating that the relationship will never be fixed without a mutual effort.

One benefit of the integrity position, I explained, is that your changes might affect the way your partner behaves. I told Cathy that if she were more assertive in her marriage, it might influence the way Jerry treated her. Maybe if she acted differently, he would change as well.

Another benefit of the integrity position is that your efforts build good faith and set a good example. This sometimes inspires partners to work on themselves.

I told Cathy that unless she wanted a divorce right away, she had everything to gain by working on herself. Even if her changes didn't save the marriage, it was still important that she learn to be assertive: (1) for her own sake, because assertiveness is an important life skill; (2) so she could hold her head high if she left the relationship, knowing she had done everything possible; and (3) so she would be prepared for future relationships and never again duplicate the same negative pattern.

Cathy saw the merit in the integrity position. She wavered for a few weeks, seriously considering divorce. Finally she decided to stay in the marriage and work both on the relationship and the rest of her personal life.

In thinking about her decision to stay, Cathy had difficulty sorting through her own motivation: Was she staying mainly because of fear? Was she staying for the kids? Was she staying because she loved Jerry? She also wondered: Did she even love Jerry anymore? Did anger mask her love, or had it extinguished it?

Cathy was concerned that she might be staying because of fear and that she might want to leave when she finally could support herself.

I told her I believed it would be impossible to precisely determine her motivation at this point. Many factors were operating at once. As time passed, she would gain clarity. Meanwhile, she could proceed in good faith, trying to improve the relationship as she worked on her own personal issues.

Right away Cathy worked hard on improving her personal life. All she needed was support and encouragement. It didn't take long before she enrolled in a community college and began studies in nursing. She gradually gained confidence. She started to believe in herself and succeed in school. She made new friends, got back in touch with old ones, and began to have fun.

From the beginning I had told Cathy that it would be good if Jerry would come to counseling with her to work on their relationship. She doubted that he would come because he was too defensive, but she asked anyway. As expected, he brushed her off. Jerry's ideas about psychology and psychologists were negative. After her appointments, he would sometimes ask, "What am I doing wrong this time?" This was ironic, because I was trying to help Cathy see her own part in the problem. She already was clear about his part, although it was true that I was also teaching her more effective ways of communicating what she felt.

Cathy was only minimally successful in her efforts to maintain the integrity position on the home front. She was very angry at Jerry and saw him in a terribly negative light. He was an oppressor. He was selfish. He was cruel. He had to control everything. I sympathized in that Jerry didn't seem to want to work on his problems, but reminded her that she needed to work on her part of it. Although she had become more assertive about an independent life, she was passive and quietly angry about the situation at home. She did not always say what she wanted, but then would accuse Jerry of trying to control her.

Cathy told me about a recent time during which she felt Jerry had controlled her. She was hinting to him about inviting her friend Susan to their home. Jerry called Susan "an uptown snob" and said how much he despised her.

"See," Cathy said, "he won't let me invite my friends to the house. It makes me so angry."

"But," I answered, "you never told him that you wanted her to come. You never directly said what you wanted. Just because he called your friend a name doesn't mean that you can't invite her."

Certainly Cathy didn't like Jerry's attitude. But still he had not prevented her from inviting her friend to visit. In this case she needed to be more assertive to tell Jerry (1) that she would like him to stop insulting her friends and (2) that she wanted to invite Susan to their home.

INNER OBSTACLES

Cathy recognized the importance of becoming more assertive. Yet she knew her role model was her mother, who had always deferred to her father and who had been harassed when she stood up to him.

Cathy's childhood experiences also worked against assertiveness. She had been warned over and over again not to be selfish. Invariably she was accused of being selfish when she would assert herself in the family. She learned she shouldn't ask for what she wanted. Her needs and feelings were discounted.

Another obstacle to Cathy's assertiveness was fear of responsibility. For instance, Cathy had avoided responsibility for paying credit card bills because she was afraid she would make mistakes. In particular, Cathy was scared to take a strong stand. If, for example, she said where she wanted to go on vacation and the trip flopped, she didn't want to be held responsible. Her fear was fueled by lack of self-confidence and a history of being criticized by parents and now by her husband.

Clearly Cathy had learned a pattern of behavior as a child that she carried over to her adult relationships. This pattern is called a *relationship script*. Based on childhood experiences, her behavior in a relationship was predictable, as if she were reading a theatrical script. With little self-confidence and little self-esteem, Cathy struggled to win approval, putting aside her own needs, and trying to find someone who would take care of her. She had found Jerry, who fit the bill. But she resented his control.

A HISTORY OF NOT NEGOTIATING

After about three months of counseling, Cathy was finally able to convince Jerry to come with her. Jerry turned out to be a very likeable guy, much kinder than you would expect if you had listened uncritically to Cathy's complaints. During the first session together, Jerry gave his perspective on their problems. First, he said he had been happy with their marriage and thought Cathy had been happy, too, until recently. They were doing fine financially and were raising two wonderful children. But now it seemed that Cathy was "on the warpath":

"Now she tells me I'm cold and unloving. I hate that. It makes me crazy."

It was clear that until recently he didn't have a clue about the extent of Cathy's unhappiness. Their marriage could easily have ended as a classic example of the big surprise, with Cathy suddenly leaving and Jerry being caught totally off guard. I believe that Cathy would have left if it weren't for the children.

Jerry admitted that there had been some things in the marriage that bothered him all along, but said he had accepted them. He talked about the way Cathy depended on him for everything, and that this responsibility was a big burden.

As the session progressed, Cathy said she wanted to settle an argument from the proceeding week. She had told Jerry just recently about her decision to vacuum the carpets only once a week. Jerry complained that the carpets were filthy and called her a slob, and then wouldn't talk to her for three days.

"This is what makes me so mad," Cathy said. "Everything's got to be your way. If I do what I want to do, you call me names and give me the silent treatment. You don't know how to be loving. You're totally selfish."

"No," he answered, "*you're* selfish. You picked a time I was under a great deal of pressure at work to stop cleaning our house. I value a clean house, and you know it. It's especially important to me when I'm under stress. You didn't even ask my opinion. You just went ahead and did it."

"You're all caught up in yourself," she said. "You're always under pressure. You don't care about anyone else. You go around trying to run everybody's life. You're bossy. You've got to make all the decisions."

"You know perfectly well that I take good care of you. If I'm so bad, then I don't know why you stay with me."

To defuse the tension, I explained that they were arguing over an issue that every couple must confront: the division of labor. Many couples start as they did, with divergent ideas about standards of work and about the way it is divided. From what I had gathered, they had never had a thorough, detailed discussion to settle this matter. Consequently they argued about housework on a day-by-day basis. I told them that this was an important part of their problem.

The challenge, I added, was to find agreements that both of them felt were reasonable and fair. And, I said, when good agreements are *not* in place, arguments tend to erupt at the least desirable moments, and often when people are under a great deal of stress. Because they were stuck, and had never settled the division of labor, this dispute had remained a regular source of tension between them. "It's hard to feel like a team," I said, "if you don't talk things through and settle your differences."

I also explained that conflict must be brought into the open in a relationship, with a cooperative spirit. Then couples can settle their differences through reasoned discussion and negotiation. Neither Cathy nor Jerry had experienced a good role model for cooperation or for negotiation as they grew up. They needed a cooperative vision.

I suggested that we could work together as a team the following week to establish agreements about the division of labor and the standards of household cleanliness. They left the session with what appeared to be goodwill, and a sense of hope that something could be done.

But there was no Jerry next week. Cathy came alone. Apparently Jerry had been angry at her all week for saying bad things about him in counseling. He didn't come back because he felt that I had excused Cathy's inexcusable behavior (her unilateral decision about the carpets). Knowing how critical and negative Jerry could be, it wasn't surprising that he found fault with me. And the fact that he found it inexcusable that Cathy had not vacuumed the carpet sounded like a classic example of "lover's panic"—interpreting a small problem in a way that made it seem enormous.

I didn't see Jerry for about six months. Meanwhile, Cathy more or less stuck to the integrity position. She continued to thrive in school and with friends. As she felt stronger, she stopped doing much of the work that Jerry had demanded, and resisted or dragged her feet on parts of it. She stopped being so obedient. She also started asking for more of what she wanted from Jerry, especially in terms of help with housework and raising the children, and time to be with her friends. Still, she said, he was trying hard to control her. She said that he seemed to be getting worse, more cruel and controlling, as if he couldn't tolerate her sense of independence or good feelings about herself. Jerry resented Cathy's increased absence from the home and the increased demands for his help with the children.

About six months after our first meeting, Jerry was back in my office—alone. He had been drinking more than he should after work and on weekends. He was basically unhappy and depressed. And as I knew, his marriage had become a source of stress.

Through my sessions with him, I got to know more of his personal history. Just like Cathy, he had a strong need for approval. This could be traced to an upbringing in which winning approval was so tenuous. On the one hand, his parents would pressure him to succeed, even as they told him he was "a loser" who would never amount to anything. On the other hand, when he did succeed at something, they ridiculed him and said it wouldn't last.

Jerry had one poignant childhood memory of his parents' attitude to his success: When he played on an all-star soccer team in fifth grade, they said they would go to the game but they expected him to embarrass them. He was very hurt.

Jerry's father had a serious gambling problem and a bad temper. As a child, Jerry never wanted to bring friends home because he was embarrassed by his father's behavior. Many of Jerry's peers made fun of his father and his family. The combined effect of parents who neglected and criticized him and of peers who ridiculed him was to leave Jerry feeling: "You can't count on people. They will disappoint and hurt you."

After doing well in junior high school, Jerry gave up in high school. He remembers thinking, "I don't care." He stopped studying and doing his homework. He played the guitar, smoked a lot of marijuana, and drank beer. He felt like a loser. In spite of a lack of motivation, he was bright and still managed to graduate from high school.

Shortly after graduating, he started working at an entry-level job for the cable television company. At that time, he happened to read a book on leadership and success that struck a chord. This book stressed the importance of working hard, maintaining a competitive edge, and "never letting anyone gain the upper hand." Jerry started striving for success and began to climb the corporate ladder. He found a way of life that worked: a ruthless dedication to self-interest and details. He became almost compulsive in his work habits and managed to stay in control in almost all work situations. He tasted success and liked it.

One time when his parents visited to see him receive an award for "employee of the year," Jerry expected praise. But when they saw him at the podium, they laughed and said, "Let's see how long this lasts."

FALSE POWER

Soon I began to meet with Jerry and Cathy as a couple. The history of their relationship was easy to piece together. The initial problem was an imbalance of power. Out of their own personal insecurities, Jerry was controlling and Cathy was dependent. The more dependent she was, the more he took over. The more he took over, the more dependent she became. At first neither of them had problems with this arrangement. It compensated for their self-esteem problems. He needed to be in control. She felt helpless and needed someone to take control. Over time, Cathy started feeling resentful about the arrangement, asking questions such as: "Why does he always do things his way? Why do I always have to give in? Doesn't he care about me? What about my feelings?" On the issue of a social life she asked: "Why can't I see my friends?" About housework: "Why do I have to walk on eggshells?" As she asked these questions, she started knocking him off the pedestal: "He is so selfish, self-centered. He is like a bully."

All along Jerry worked hard to provide for the family. As Cathy criticized him, it reinforced his belief that life is unfair and people untrustworthy. He thought: "How can Cathy view me in such a negative light? How can she call me selfish?" From his point of view, this was outrageous.

Jerry's survival-based thinking, which worked when peers picked on him in school and also helped him move up the corporate ladder, was never to yield an inch to a challenger. It would be like admitting defeat. So when Cathy protested about something, Jerry was unyielding and struck back with force, sometimes in insulting ways and sometimes by giving her the silent treatment.

I call Jerry's attack on Cathy *false power*. People often use false power when they believe they have been wronged. On these occasions they say to themselves that they have been so grievously mistreated that they must intervene with strong action, right away, to correct the matter. At that moment they use whatever power plays they believe will be effective.

False power sometimes intimidates a partner temporarily but never works in restoring a relationship to a positive footing. In Jerry's case the more he resorted to power plays, the angrier and more defiant Cathy became.

It is easy to show this. One time Cathy said he was "lazy and getting flabby because he wasn't exercising." Worse still, she said it in front of the children. Jerry had a valid gripe and felt humiliated. But he went on a rampage, calling Cathy one name after another. Then he didn't talk to her for a few days. I asked Jerry why he did this. He said, "I just got so mad. Somehow I wanted to get through. I wanted to reach her."

"Did it work?"

"No."

"Have you reacted this way before?"

"Yes."

"Has it ever worked?"

"No. Cathy just starts calling me a cruel husband. She gets angrier and more vengeful."

That's the problem. False power doesn't work. In fact, it backfires by creating more resistance. Yet people resort to false power over and over again, always believing that it will fix a problem. The real challenge for Jerry was to appeal to Cathy's sense of reason and good judgment. That's the only way the two of them could successfully work out their problems.

OVERCOMING COMPETITIVE CONDITIONING

Cathy and Jerry seemed to accept the cooperative vision. They wanted to share power and become a team. But they, like the rest of us, were trained to compete in one way or another. In a competitive society, people internalize a variety of messages that are counter to cooperation. These messages center on giving away power (don't ask for what you want); mistrust (you won't be loved); and grabbing power (better watch out for yourself; don't let the other person get away with anything).

An awareness of the cooperative vision opens up possibilities. People can begin to confront their own competitive training as they learn new cooperative skills. But the process is not fast. We have layer upon layer of competitive training to overcome.

Cathy and Jerry persisted in trying to learn to cooperate, but often they arrived at the same stumbling blocks. Sometimes people have to see the same pattern repeatedly in different situations until they finally understand what's happening and the ways in which they must change.

Cathy was taking small steps forward as she began to ask Jerry to do some of the social activities she enjoyed. But problems would occur. One example was when they planned to meet another couple for dinner.

Fifteen minutes before they were supposed to leave for the restaurant, Jerry started working on an electrical repair in the kitchen. Cathy was annoyed and, knowing Jerry's lack of handyman ability, assumed it would be a long project. Sure enough, when it was time to leave, he was still in his work clothes. She entered the kitchen and stood over him quietly. Then she left for a few minutes and came back and did the same thing.

"Why are you just standing there?" he asked.

"Well, we're supposed to meet our friends for dinner at eight. Did you forget?"

"No, I didn't. Why don't you go without me. I'll get there as fast as I can. I didn't think this job would take so long, and now the electricity is off. I need to finish it."

"You're so selfish. Don't you care about anyone else but yourself," Cathy said as she left, annoyed.

When Jerry joined Cathy and their friends, about forty minutes later, he was noticeably angry, and rude to everyone. He gave Cathy dirty looks, and then ignored her for three days. Cathy was hurt and resentful.

We discussed the situation in counseling. It was good that Cathy asked Jerry to go to dinner. But she did not directly express her concern when he started working on the project, and annoyance when he wasn't ready to leave ("because I would never hear the end of it"). She also didn't say what she felt and what she wanted when she stood over him in the kitchen. ("I'd never hear the end of that, either. I knew that he didn't really want to come. I felt responsible. I was making him unhappy by asking him to have dinner with us.") Instead of directly and assertively expressing what she felt while it was happening, Cathy channeled her resentment into a parting shot, the type of hostile remark that would always set Jerry off.

Jerry was understandably annoyed by Cathy's parting shot and by the way she stood over him while he worked. But obviously he shouldn't have started a project when they had a social engagement in a few minutes. He had made a mistake.

Jerry felt wounded and believed that he had been treated unfairly when Cathy called him selfish. Matters got worse when he became aggressive and offensive in his response. More false power, and with a predictable result: Cathy felt unloved and called him a cruel husband. She was angry.

I reminded them of their respective roles in the problem. "If you want to make it work, you both have to stay out of your roles." Cathy had to ask for what she wanted. She had to express her resentment in disciplined ways, without name-calling. Jerry had to meet Cathy halfway and stop his overreactive, aggressive attacks. They each had to stop focusing on the other person's wrongdoing. When either of them was hurt, they needed to say so calmly. They needed to stop locking horns: She shouldn't call him unloving. He shouldn't get aggressive.

Over the course of several sessions we talked about disciplined ways of expressing negative feelings such as hurt and resentment. Neither of them had role models of loving, cooperative communication. It was important that they learn ways of expressing their negative feelings without attacking each other.

WHEN COOPERATION AND NEGOTIATIONS FAIL

Cathy and Jerry kept working on their relationship. For short periods of time they would appear to be making progress. Cathy would assertively ask for what she wanted. Jerry would listen and negotiate. Jerry would keep his temper under control. Cathy would calm her anger. Neither would attack the other.

But almost every week, something would go wrong. By the end of the week, Cathy would be saying, "I can't ask for what I want. He just wants to control me. He went off on one of his rampages." Jerry would say, "I can't do anything right in her eyes. She always sees me as cruel. She doesn't even say what she wants and then gets angry at me."

At first it was easy to be patient with the process. It takes time to overcome bad habits that were learned mostly in childhood. With each setback Cathy and Jerry would renew their commitments to change. Cathy said she would ask for what she wanted and stop agreeing to do things she didn't want to do. Jerry would listen to Cathy's point of view, negotiate reasonably, make compromises, and stop his aggressive attacks. But with all their continued commitment, they still didn't seem to be able to make and keep cooperative agreements. The problems persisted. They were not mastering the art of maintaining a loving, cooperative relationship. Instead they were mired in a competitive mode. This, then, became the focus of my interventions.

I warned that there was little hope for the relationship unless Cathy stopped being so dependent and angry, and Jerry stopped being so controlling and nasty. Neither of them seemed to trust the other. Neither cut any slack for the other.

CHILDHOOD INFLUENCES

I talked with Cathy and Jerry about the ways in which they continued to make some of the same mistakes over and over again. I pointed out that the two of them always seemed to arrive at the same feeling states.

Cathy felt she was unloved, and needed to accommodate Jerry to win his approval. In the old days, she accommodated, but resented it. Nowadays she rebelled, but resented it. Regardless, she felt she was not being loved. She was hurt. She was angry.

Jerry felt he was being treated unfairly. Cathy was letting him down. He was not appreciated, and no matter how hard he tried, he could never win her approval. Jerry learned to defend himself against perceived mistreatment by getting aggressive and never yielding.

Their horns were locked: When Cathy felt unloved, she attacked Jerry. When Jerry felt under attack, he counterattacked in a very aggressive way. This made Cathy feel more unloved, and the cycle kept going.

In separate sessions, I began talking with each of them about these recurring feelings.

I asked them some of the basic questions people need to ask themselves when trying to identify negative childhood influences in a relationship:

"What do you usually feel when you are having troubles in your relationship?"

Cathy said she felt unloved and angry.

Jerry said he felt hurt and angry.

"Have you ever felt those feeling before? Are they familiar? Did you feel them in other relationships?"

Both remembered these feelings from previous romantic relationships.

"When do you first remember feeling those feelings? What was the situation?"

Both of them pointed to early childhood experiences in their families.

Cathy was aware of trying to win the approval of her father, of being quiet about her needs, and of resenting him. She did not trust men. She didn't feel loved. Jerry remembered his sense of hopelessness about gaining approval from his parents, his anger about it, and his determination to fight against the injustices. He didn't trust people. He felt let down by people.

Both Jerry and Cathy had a sense of feeling unlovable, and a fear that no one would love them.

Now, as adults, the two of them were reliving their childhood training. It was clear that they had to take a hard look at their own history to make changes in the present. Somehow they had to recognize that the powerful feelings of hurt, fear, and anger that originated in their childhood were still operating and damaging their marriage.

It was an issue of the ability to love and to trust. They had to overcome powerful early training that conditioned them to expect that they would be mistreated and unloved. To move forward, they had to give affirmative answers to these questions: Can you keep focused on what is fine and wonderful in your partner? Do you want your partner to be happy? Do you want to be part of a team? Can you trust that you will be loved?

FIGHTING MONSTERS

Raising the question about their own ability to love motivated Jerry to face something that was hard to face. As much as he hated Cathy telling him that he was cruel to her, he did feel that sometimes he would be cruel to her. He said he hated this about himself, and assured me that in general he was good to his family. This I knew to be true.

Jerry had previously talked about losing his temper. But this time he was admitting the frequency of what he was doing, and that he felt out of control. He said it felt to him as if monsters took over, getting him to do things he didn't want to do. When he got nasty, he knew he would feel bad later, but still he could not quite control himself.

Of course, I told him, there are no monsters. So something must be happening that caused him to lose control. As we talked he realized that he would lose control when he was under large amounts of stress (a frequent occurrence for a man with two children, a problem marriage, and a corporate job) and when he was criticized by Cathy. On these occasions he began to feel alienated—all alone—and disconnected from his family. It was "me against the world." That was his familiar state of being, learned as a child in a heartless family. When he felt this way, he would lash out at Cathy and the children.

Jerry didn't recognize the stress as it occurred. But his brilliant insight about lashing out offered promise for his relationship. He needed to learn to monitor himself for feelings of stress. He needed to learn to calm himself when he was criticized. And on these occasions he had to remind himself that he was not a small child in a heartless world. He was a member of a family. He would only make matters worse if he antagonized the people he loved. He needed to pull together with them as a team.

This was a big breakthrough. Jerry gained an enormous amount of self-control from this understanding, which enabled him to blaze a positive course in the marriage. As his aggressive barrages decreased, Cathy started feeling safer and was finally able to master some of the assertive skills that had eluded her.

Cathy started to make great progress when she stopped seeing herself as a victim and Jerry as the source of all her problems. More and more she could see her own collusion in powerlessness. She saw how she had given away power and attempted to win Jerry's approval by doing whatever he wanted her to do. This was exactly what she had done with her own father as a child. She saw that she gained nothing by attacking

Jerry and blaming him for everything. She recognized that she needed to grow up and that she had everything to gain by becoming more assertive.

More important, she was able to see Jerry without a cloud of her own distortions. Surely he had problems, but Cathy could now see his wonderful qualities. It felt good to see what she liked in her husband and to feel some warmth again, the warmth she had feared never would return. Gradually Jerry's distortions also diminished. He came to recognize how joyful, affectionate, and trustworthy Cathy could be. He stopped feeling so much hurt, and began to feel loved. He started to trust Cathy.

Cathy changed her college major from nursing and is now working as a counselor, fulfilling her dream of helping children who come from troubled homes. Jerry is an upper-level manager.

The two of them made it. Both of them changed at the same time. Little by little they continued to overcome childhood influences that had programed them for roles of dominance and submission. They learned to share power and settle differences openly, through dialogue, and with love. They are much happier people now, no longer guided by negative, antiquated scripts from their difficult childhoods. At this time they are enjoying a wonderful love story that they wrote for themselves.

CHAPTER
12

Glossary/Summary of Ideas

Now you have read the love stories and seen how hard it is for a couple to share power cooperatively. We all want good relationships. We start with high hopes. But most of us start with handicaps:
1. We have learned to feel comfortable on top, or on bottom, or in a struggle for the top.
2. We lack a vision of cooperation and of how to share power as equals, especially when the going gets rough.
3. Even among those of us aware of the cooperative option, most lack the skills to share power and keep each other happy.

These handicaps lead to power struggles and power imbalances that undermine the ability of a couple to maintain their loving feelings. Couples who are unable to find cooperative solutions to their problems eventually are torn apart by a cycle of hurt, mistrust, and anger.

Conflict is inevitable. Even the most loving people in the most compatible relationships have conflict. People always have differences. The important issue is how couples express and resolve their differences.

In the heat of an argument, people tend to forget that they care about their partners. They forget that their partners care about them. They forget that the essence of a loving relationship is to make each other happy. They often resort to power plays in an effort to get what they want.

Power plays are the tactics used for control and domination in a relationship, as people try to get their own way by coercing or manipulating their partners. Power plays can be subtle or overt. They are often motivated by fear and mistrust: People are afraid that they'll be cheated if they don't push hard for themselves. Sometimes power plays are deliberate and conscious attempts to dominate; at other times they're an automatic, unconscious response to conflict.

Some people try to avoid conflict completely in their relationships. They make peace at any price, often by rescuing their partners.

Rescuing. Rescuing means to put aside one's own thoughts, feelings, and desires to save (or rescue) a partner from having to deal with them. People who rescue usually have been told to be "nice" and "loving" and to take care of other people first. They also have been told that asserting their own needs would be selfish. So they give away their power. The result is one-sided relationships that are not really loving, because most of the affection is going in only one direction. This imbalance undermines good feelings and eventually leads to resentment and a fierce power struggle.

Rescuing behavior is frequently misperceived as cooperative. However, "giving in" to a partner is not a cooperative option if an attempt wasn't first made to find a solution that would fully satisfy everyone. It's also not a cooperative option if the same person almost always makes the concessions. Such an imbalance indicates a lack of mutual respect.

The big surprise. Rescuing is an emotional time bomb. People tolerate being on the bottom only so long before they finally explode.

Most people who rescue resent the lack of reciprocation from their partners, and may at times express their feelings through sarcasm or unexplainable outbursts over minor incidents. Sooner or later the hurt and resentment grow to crisis proportions.

In desperation, the hurt and now very angry person may resort to dramatic actions, such as having an affair, threatening to file for a divorce, or actually file for one. At this point, their partners are flabbergasted. Because the hurt and angry feelings had been hidden, the partner didn't anticipate a problem. So the sudden change is called the big surprise. However, it isn't surprising at all. People who don't assert their needs and don't do anything about situations that feel bad are likely to become dissatisfied in a major way. It's just a matter of time.

The cooperative vision. To succeed in a relationship we must transcend all our cultural training in competitiveness. We need to change our attitudes to the core and reject the idea of being on top or on bottom in a relationship. Couples must realize that their fates are totally intermingled: It is one for all and all for one. We need to redefine conflict: If one person is unhappy, both suffer. If one person dominates, the other suffers, and so does the relationship.

A good starting point for people who want a loving relationship with equal power is to make an agreement to work as a team to meet each other's needs. A formal agreement of this sort is called a *Basic Cooperative Agreement (BCA)*. With a BCA, two individuals strive for equality. No one tries to dominate. No one accepts a subordinate position. Instead, a couple pool their energy so the whole is greater than the sum of the parts. Two people working together, in partnership, can create more benefits together than two people working alone.

Making a BCA means approaching conflict as a team. Instead of each thinking in terms of self-interest—"What is best for me?"—couples redefine conflict in a cooperative manner by asking these questions:

"How can you and I work as a team to find solutions to our differences? How can we figure things out together so that we *both* feel satisfied? What will work for us?"

This necessitates a type of cooperative negotiation that differs from the traditional adversarial, win-lose process, with each individual looking to gain a competitive edge. (With couples, win-lose conflict inevitably becomes lose-lose. Everyone gets less than he deserves.) The goal with a BCA is to find win-win, cooperative solutions to conflict.

The important implications of a basic cooperative agreement can be thought of in three main categories: attitude, communication, and conflict resolution.

ATTITUDE

The starting point for a cooperative vision and a Basic Cooperative Agreement (BCA) is a change in attitude. Because the cultural mind-set about relationships is competitive, changing one's attitude is a big challenge, requiring frequent reminders, a great deal of attention, and concentration.

Super decision. The super decision means committing oneself to a very high standard of behavior with the people we love. It means *being careful* with intense feelings, and reminding ourselves always to treat the people we love with the respect and affection we feel for them. It is a commitment to struggle against impulses to grab power or to lash out and unnecessarily hurt the people we love. We watch ourselves and use a great deal of self-discipline and self-control when we are upset.

Super challenge. When two people argue, usually each person thinks that he or she is right and the other is wrong. The super challenge is an attempt to neutralize this way of thinking. There are two parts to the super challenge:

1. Learn to question yourself. Realize that your opinion (or position) is not necessarily right, no matter how certain you are of yourself. Accept the possibility that you could be wrong. Bear in mind that the other person may be equally certain of his or her position.

2. Don't assume that the other person (your partner) is wrong. Look for validity in what your partner is saying. Your partner probably wouldn't be arguing unless that person thought he or she was right.

Super calmness. This means having enough self-control to stay cool and behave respectfully toward a partner when you are upset or in conflict. You don't get grouchy, short-tempered, or hypercritical. You don't allow yourself to get aggressive or defensive. It is important to remain calm so that cooperative communication can take place. People need to learn to calm themselves, to lower their intensity when agitated. They must be able to remind themselves of their love for their partners when they get upset. Only by remaining calm will they be able to conduct the type of disciplined discussion needed to solve problems and resolve conflict.

Relationships require commitment and work. Some people hedge their commitment to their partners. They may live together or get married, but overreact or think about quitting the relationship at the first signs of trouble, or in response to a particular shortcoming of a partner. *Lover's panic* occurs when small problems or minor incidents cause people to panic. They overgeneralize and fear they won't be loved, or that they'll be consistently hurt, disappointed, or somehow cheated or mistreated. With lover's panic, people get too upset and can't deal with little issues in an appropriate, calm way because they are so busy thinking and fearing that the whole relationship is defective.

People who suffer from lover's panic do not bear in mind (1) that all people have flaws and problems and (2) that relationships require work. You can't sit back and judge your partner and overreact to every problem. You need to commit to the partner you love (imperfections and all), and then work hard to make a better relationship.

Conflict can be mastered. With our competitive upbringing, many people have a dog-eat-dog attitude toward conflict that is totally inappropriate for couples who want to share power. Others try to sidestep conflict, leaving all their differences unresolved, but simmering beneath the surface.

Couples with a vision of sharing power as equals need to believe that they can allow their inevitable differences to surface and resolve matters in a respectful, cooperative way that preserves goodwill. They must believe in the conflict-resolving potential of loving communication and cooperative negotiation. Solutions can be found that will feel good to both parties involved.

Time, affection, and togetherness. A couple committed to a loving relationship need to devote time and energy to their endeavor. They need togetherness. They need to talk, plan, solve problems together, and make each other feel special. They can't be running off in different directions all the time and still feel close and connected.

People often do not give enough compliments and positive recognition to each other. The ability of couples to sustain their efforts when the going gets rough is, to a large extent, a function of the amount of love and affection they express to each other on a regular basis.

Consideration is an old-fashioned, often overlooked concept. Before one person adjusts the heater or air conditioner or uses the remote control clicker, it is a good idea to ask a partner how he or she feels. Lack of consideration often results in resentment and relationship problems.

Maintaining excitement in a relationship is an active process. Individuals must have fun and do creative things together. They also must have interesting lives as individuals. Otherwise their interest in one another is likely to dwindle.

COMMUNICATION

Communication skills can be terribly abused in relationships. People sometimes learn to communicate well so they can outtalk or manipulate their partners. It is *only* within the context of agreeing to cooperate with a partner and wanting to monitor oneself for proper behavior that communication becomes what I call *loving communication*. Loving communication is always directed toward promoting support, understanding, an exchange of affection, and mutual well-being.

When people agree to cooperate—when they make the super decision and a Basic Cooperative Agreement (BCA)—certain important assumptions about communication follow:
- Individuals will make every effort to express their positive, loving, and supportive feelings.
- No one will deliberately hurt anyone else.
- Each person will be committed to listening carefully to the other.
- Couples will commit to bringing conflict into the open, so it can be handled in direct and sensitive ways and settled to everybody's satisfaction.
- Couples will be careful and disciplined in communication. They will speak with respect. They will bring up problems in a loving way.
- No one will deliberately use aggressive or manipulative communication methods to try to dominate. No one will give away personal power and accept a subordinate role.

People in loving relationships want to know what their partners feel. They care about their feelings. *"I statements"* are a good way for expressing hurt, anger, and other feelings. These statements use a fill-in-the-blanks sentence format that goes like this:

When you did (A), I felt (B).

In this format, (A) describes a behavior. In describing the behavior, it is important to be specific. The more specific the speaker is in explaining the behavior, the better the chances are that the listener will understand the event being described.

In this format, (B) is a description of how the speaker feels now or felt at the time, such as angry, annoyed, hurt, sad, or scared.

Egocentrism. Egocentrism means the world centers on oneself. People see things from their own eyes, but not the eyes of others. Egocentric communication is a major obstacle to loving communication. People who communicate egocentrically send the following types of messages:
- This is what I feel. (It is the only way to look at what's happening.)
- This is what I think. (Therefore, this is the way it is.)
- My point of view is the absolute truth. (It is the only valid way to see things, and all that matters.)

An excellent way to counter an egocentric tendency is to learn to speak with a degree of humility, in unassuming ways, using phrases such as these:
- "This is my opinion . . . "
- "This is what I think . . . "
- "These are my feelings . . . "
- "It appears to me . . . "

This type of phrasing allows for another person's point of view.

It is also important always to ask what your partner is thinking or feeling. It is a good idea, in fact, either to precede your statements, or to follow them, with a question such as:
- "What do you think?"
- "What is your opinion?"
- "How do you feel about this?"

There has to be room for differences. The idea of loving communication is that all individuals say what they think and feel, so that everything is out in the open. Then negotiations can begin.

Super challenge. Self-certainty is a danger in couple relationships. The super challenge keeps you on your toes, remembering—even in the heat of an argument—that the way you see things could be wrong and that the way your partner sees things could be right.

The next step is called keeping a *super-open mind*. This means making a serious effort to understand what may be wrong about your own point of view and right about your partner's. It means that you seek and are receptive to points of view other than those you currently hold.

Perspective-taking. This means having the ability to see things from a partner's point of view. It is the opposite of egocentrism.

Negating. The process of *negating* occurs when one person ignores, dismisses, or brushes aside the feelings or opinions of the other person. By negating the other person, he or she attempts to make his or her own point of view dominant.

Sometimes people negate each other in an openly competitive spirit, in an effort to win. More often they do it automatically, without even realizing it. People are so absorbed in their own point of view that they have trouble putting themselves in their partner's frame of reference.

Constructive criticism. In relationships, you need the benefit of a partner's observations, including constructive criticism. The key word is *constructive*. The intent should be to support and build you up, not to tear you down. When relationships are really clicking, partners help each other grow by offering constructive criticism.

Below are a few general *rules of thumb for constructive criticism*.

• The tone of voice should be loving, calm, and reasonable.

• Never present criticism in an attempt to impose your will on a partner. To this end, avoid name-calling or put-downs. Stay away from extreme terms such as "always" and "never" unless they are completely accurate descriptions of what you are saying. Don't keep repeating yourself.

- Be as specific as possible so that your partner knows what you are talking about. If you make generalizations, also give specifics.
- Be sure to distinguish fact from opinion.

Heartfelt apologies. People sometimes hurt the people they love. When there is a cooperative spirit, it is important to give heartfelt apologies. These apologies differ completely from formal, insincere apologies, which involve uttering the words "I'm sorry" without caring about the other person's feelings. Cooperative, heartfelt apologies are sincere. When you have hurt someone you love, you take responsibility for the pain you have caused and want to help that person.

The quickest way to resolve an argument successfully is to make a sincere apology for your own wrongdoing, even if you feel your partner also has done wrong.

Good listening skills. Listening is a lost art in a competitive world. People too often listen with a spirit of competition, contemplating how to pick apart a partner's argument and preparing answers while the other person is still speaking. People listen in fear and mistrust and often misinterpret what is being said. Below are three techniques to improve listening skills:

1. Remind yourself of the purpose and benefits of loving communication within the context of a Basic Cooperative Agreement. You can think of it this way:

"I am building a loving, cooperative relationship. I don't give up power by listening, because no one is trying to dominate me. I can listen even to strong feelings and strong criticism without being threatened and without losing power. I will gain understanding. Even if I don't like what is being said, and don't agree, I will better understand my partner's point of view. That will help us reconcile our differences. I will have an opportunity to speak later."

2. *The pause.* Take a moment to pause before responding. During this time, listeners can calm themselves, and think about what was said. The pause counteracts a natural tendency

to become defensive and quickly reject an "opposing" point of view.

3. *Paraphrasing*. This means to say back what was said in different words to make sure that you understand the communication. When you paraphrase, you don't agree, disagree, or challenge. It is just a reality check to be sure you understand what was said.

The concept of *on-track and off-track* discussions is important for people who want to communicate cooperatively. The goal of a loving, cooperative relationship is to work together to satisfy each other.

In this context, communication is on track when it promotes understanding, affection, and teamwork. It is on track when it helps individuals respectfully clarify and resolve their differences, without either person dominating or accepting a subservient position. It is on track when it helps a couple solve problems together.

Communication is off track when people use their words in unnecessarily hurtful, or competitive and selfish, ways. Also, communication is off track when one person accepts a subservient position.

If couples want good discussions, they have to focus on staying on track, and monitor their efforts. By watching closely, couples can develop a sense of what is on track and what is not.

The model for an on-track discussion goes like this:
- These are my thoughts. What are yours?
- These are my feelings. What are yours?
- This is what I want. What do you want?
- Let's see where we agree. Let's try to understand our differences. Then let's talk about our differences and reach an agreement.
- What are your ideas about resolving our differences? These are my ideas. What do you think?

To stay on track, couples need self-awareness (individuals need to know what they think and feel); self-discipline (speaking clearly and carefully, in nonthreatening ways); listening skills (taking one's partner seriously, without negating or discounting); focus (solving one problem at a time without spilling into other problems); flexibility (handling related problems, but one at a time); and reason and fairness as priorities (rejecting power-based relationships).

A basic principle of on-track discussions is the following:

When one person is off track, there is still hope. When both people are off track, they're going to have a fight.

When people think their partners are off track, they need to use *super discipline* to rise above the perceived errors so they can redirect a discussion back on track.

When you feel wronged, super discipline means to explain calmly what you think and feel, with care, remembering that the purpose of communication in a cooperative relationship is to love and support each other. You do not allow yourself to get overcome with emotions. You do not resort to statements that would further veer the discussion off track. *Tolerance* means accepting that a partner sometimes makes mistakes. Tolerance increases people's capacity to respond calmly, in a disciplined manner, when they believe they have been wronged.

I call it *false power* whenever people in loving relationships get the idea that a power play can quickly correct an injustice. People who believe they have been "wronged" justify their own abuses of power as an attempt to correct the wrongdoing of others. People huff and puff with false power but only make matters worse.

Couple communication breaks down at the *stuck point*. This is the moment at which discussions that should continue, instead stop. The discussion ends prematurely, without resolution. Because the conflict is never resolved, the same types of fights recur, ending each time at the same or similar stuck points.

The key to success in cooperative relationships is never allowing the dialogue to end without getting to the bottom of the problem. Couples need to be able to identify the way in which they get stuck so they can move toward solutions.

CONFLICT RESOLUTION

Conflict is part of life and part of relationships. People who want to share power as equals need to learn to negotiate cooperatively, and to solve the complex problems that cause them to lock horns.

Wisdom of the sunset couples. Couples who have been happily married for many years acknowledge that they went through tough times during their early years together. But they faced their problems and engaged in discussions that continued until they found solutions that worked for both individuals. They faced their differences and kept talking until the conflict was resolved.

Cooperative negotiation is an alternative to the conventional connotation of negotiating, which involves people in adversarial positions bargaining with their own self-interests as primary. People in love relationships with a Basic Cooperative Agreement are not selfishly looking out for themselves. They are seeking solutions that work all around for both people. They are *finding solutions together*.

Solutions should not be "my way" or "your way." They should always be "our way." Cooperative resolution to conflict begins when each person takes the other's feelings seriously.

There are three basic ways to settle differences cooperatively:

You find a *compromise* that is acceptable all around. You make *trade-offs*: your way this time and my way next time. Or you find *creative solutions*, such that each person is satisfied without substantial concessions.

Certain *guidelines* are helpful in striving for *cooperative solutions* to conflict.

1. Say what you think and feel. This means keeping no secrets. It includes asking for 100 percent of what you want; saying what bothers you; and saying what feels good. This guideline precludes *self-bargaining*, which means making con-

cessions before negotiations begin, thereby depriving oneself of full representation during the negotiating process (and depriving a partner of an opportunity to satisfy one's needs).

2. No rescues: Don't give away your power. No power plays: Don't grab power and try to dominate.

In our culture, we are "wired" for competition. Agreeing to this guideline doesn't mean that couples will immediately master the art of cooperation. Rather, it means they understand that rescues and power plays are impediments to cooperation. They agree to be alert to these behaviors and to work toward reducing their prevalence. They commit themselves to scrutinizing their own and each other's behavior constructively. They point out when they think a partner is rescuing or using a power play. And they take responsibility for their own behavior when they find themselves rescuing or abusing power.

3. Listen to each other, and then negotiate with equality and fairness in mind.

About the cooperative negotiation process. The *process* of handling conflict in a relationship is as important as the *outcome*. This applies to negotiations as much as anything else.

You begin to negotiate by both persons saying what they want. This means that soul-searching—knowing what you want—is a prerequisite for successful negotiations. You must know yourself before you can succeed in negotiating with another person. Preferences should be stated in the most non-threatening ways possible: Fear is the enemy of dialogue and discussion. Nothing should be pushed on the other person. The idea is to find a solution that works for everyone.

Before moving to the next stage of negotiations, you must make sure everything is in the open. Ask each other: "Did you say everything you needed to say about what you want and how you feel?"

Once everything is in the open, the two people can see if their preferences are the same. If not, they begin to look for creative solutions to their differences. If they can't find one, it becomes a matter of making offers and counteroffers. In other words, someone makes a proposal or series of proposals about how to settle the matter. The offers should be compromises (meeting each other halfway) or trade-offs (your way this time, my way next time), presented in the cooperative spirit of give-and-take, as in:

"These are my ideas about how to settle our differences. What do you think?"

It is important always to ask a partner for proposals:

"What are your suggestions? What's your opinion?"

In the give-and-take process, some people tend to give too much. They *confuse concessions with compromises:* "Marriages are compromises," they say. "You don't always get what you want." Using this as a rationale, they make all or most of the concessions without asking their partner to make equivalent offers. If concessions are necessary, there should always be a balance, with each person giving equally.

Cooperating couples engage in this give-and-take process of proposing action plans until one is selected. Before committing to the agreement, both people must be satisfied with the outcome, and satisfied that the process was fair and reasonable.

A good test of the validity of an agreement is to see if both people can smile at each other after it is made. If not, something is probably wrong with the process or the outcome, and the couple needs to go back to the negotiating table.

Couples should feel closer to each other after they have negotiated than they did before: "If you feel annoyed, something is amiss."

When agreements are eventually finalized, it is a good practice to set a time in the future to review progress: to evaluate how the agreements are working and to determine if modifications are required. Couples also need a mechanism for bringing up problems with their agreements as they go along.

In negotiating cooperatively, it is important to avoid making *invalid agreements*. These are agreements that do not *really* feel satisfactory to one person. Often they are made to settle conflict quickly, and often by submissive people to get dominant people off their back. But these agreements are not true commitments. Sometimes people make them without any intention of following through. More often, people make them under duress, believing that they will comply. But their heart isn't in it. They either ignore or quickly forget the agreements, or comply for short periods of time before casting them aside.

Preventing the "big surprise." You cannot negotiate cooperatively with a partner who (1) doesn't ask for what he or she wants or (2) doesn't express criticism, resentment, or other negative feelings. Such rescuing undermines cooperation and may lead to the big surprise in which a partner suddenly erupts in unforgiving anger about the long-standing unfairness of the relationship.

The way to avoid the big surprise is by *paying attention to your partner.* You can take preventive measures, such as insisting that your partner consistently state his or her preferences before decisions are made.

Also, you should be sure that your partner feels free to express criticism and negative feelings. If these thoughts and feelings are withheld, you need to actively encourage that they be communicated.

A more positive way to think about preventing the big surprise is as follows: If you consistently pay lots of loving attention to your partner, check how he or she is doing on a regular basis, and know for a fact that he or she is happy, then you'll never be surprised by an enraged partner who had been dissatisfied for a long time. One way to keep tabs is regularly to ask your partner questions such as these: "What do you feel? What do you want? Is anything bothering you? How can I make you happier? How can we make the relationship better?"

Conflict reminders to yourself. Because of our competitive upbringing, it is really important to be able to remind yourself of certain considerations when trying to resolve conflict with a partner:

Partnership

- You love your partner.
- Your partner loves you.
- You're on the same side. You're working together.

Communication

- People who love each other should communicate in a loving, disciplined, and respectful way.
- It is important to understand and respect each other's thoughts and feelings.
- It is important to hear each other's point of view and to clarify differences.

Humility

- As certain as you may be about the correctness of your own point of view, you still could be wrong or partially wrong. Your partner could be right.
- You both could be right. You both could be wrong.
- You might be misunderstanding your partner.

The Cooperative Process

- There is a cooperative process that allows people to settle their differences with fairness and goodwill.
- You don't have to be scared. You don't have to fight. With the Basic Cooperative Agreement, no one wants to dominate. The goal is to take care of each other.
- People who work as a team and talk calmly, with love, can find solutions to problems that are acceptable to both individuals.

Huddling up is one way to think about sticking together during conflict. A couple can pull together by cuing themselves with thoughts such as these: "We love each other. We need to calm down and huddle up as a team. We need to find solutions that work for both of us. If we calm down, we will settle our differences and both feel good."

Cheering up the team. After settling an argument, it is especially important to repair the mood, for a couple to get close and help each other heal. Both partners should take responsibility for this often overlooked task.

Couples who cannot share power as equals invariably *lock horns* in conflicts they cannot resolve.

I call it locking horns when: Each person is very much bothered by what the other one is doing. Yet each is doing something that reinforces exactly what he or she doesn't like. It's a vicious circle. For example: The more critical one person is of a partner, the more defensive the partner becomes. When that person becomes defensive, the first one gets even more critical . . . and on and on and on.

This type of stalemate actually represents a peculiar power problem, a breakdown of negotiations. Each person is trying to get what he or she wants by insisting that the partner should do something different. The more each person insists that the other one should do all the changing, the deeper the problem becomes. Neither realizes that the only way to solve the problem would be by both sides making concessions, ideally at the same time. To succeed requires a creative vision and a cooperative solution. Neither person could solve the problem alone. Both have to change, and neither is likely to sustain change unless the other works on making parallel changes.

Ideally both partners change simultaneously. But you don't have to wait for a partner to change. You can be a *love leader*. The super decision is a commitment to self-improvement. Instead of playing "you go first" with a partner, you can be self-critical, discover your own part of the relationship problem, and work on it. This means that you must admit you have played a significant, contributing role in locking horns. Then you do something about it.

If you want to improve a relationship, your part of the problem is the only part you can control. You can improve on your own end and perhaps inspire your partner to make similar changes. In fact, the best way to get your partner to admit to problems is to be willing to admit your own. Ultimately you need your partner to start working on his or her end of the problem to break the pattern fully. Then both people must stay vigilantly focused on self-improvement, even when one person occasionally falters.

The downward-spiraling cycle that occurs when couples lock horns is motored, in part, by *automatic thinking*. People expect certain behavior from their partner—the old pattern they are trying to change. Without consciously realizing it, they look for what they expect and fail to notice changes.

I recommend the *integrity position* to people who want to fix or might want to fix their troubled relationships but are not sure their partner will be willing to change, and are uncertain whether the closeness and love they once felt could ever return.

With the integrity position, a person works on his or her own contribution to the relationship problem. At the same time, the person insists that the problem is "two way" and cannot possibly be resolved without a partner's participation. If the partner eventually makes changes, the relationship may improve. If the partner does not participate, the person who has maintained the integrity position knows where he stands. If he chooses, he can leave with his head held high, knowing he has done all he could to try to improve the relationship.

When people are willing to be self-critical and work on themselves, their partners often follow the lead. The missing link in most cases has been a vision of how to proceed, an understanding that people can share power as equals and create wonderful, mutually satisfying relationships. I hope you share this vision and choose to apply the attitudes and skills that have been portrayed in the love stories in this book. We humans really can love one another and keep each other happy. Couple relationships can be a great source of joy.

About the Author

Robert Schwebel, Ph.D., holds a doctorate in clinical psychology from the University of California at Berkeley. He lectures widely, has a private practice in psychology, often working with couples, and is the Clinical Director of Alcohol and Other Drug Services at Desert Hills Center for Youth and Females. He has written a weekly column about families and relationships for *The Arizona Daily Star*, and has hosted a local NBC-TV talk show about relationships, "Good Loving." He is the author of *Saying No Is Not Enough: Raising Children Who Make Wise Decisions About Drugs and Alcohol* and coauthor of *A Guide to a Happier Family*. He lives with his wife and two children in Tucson, Arizona.